London
A Pictorial History

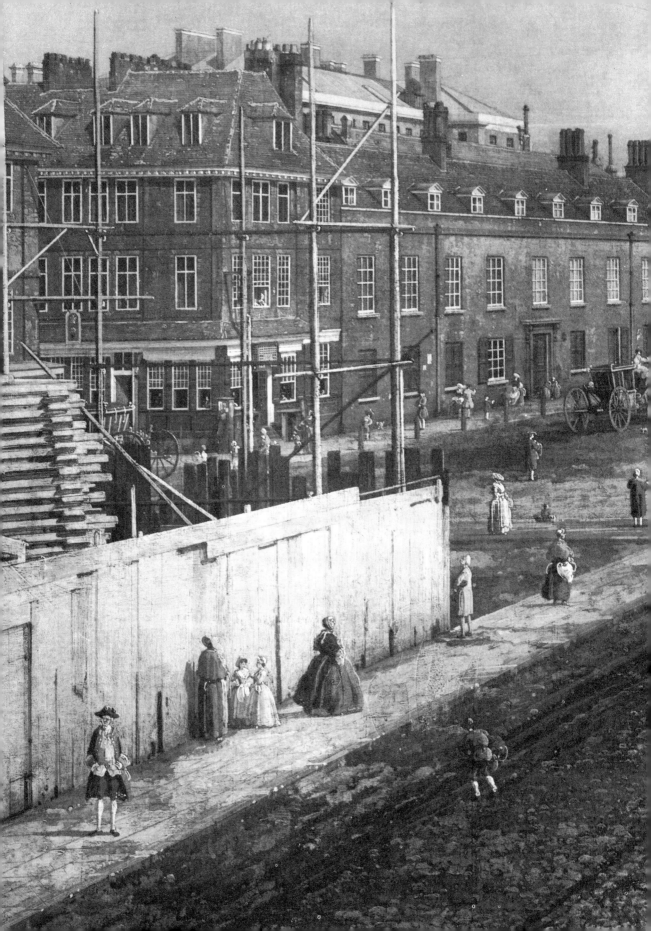

London

A Pictorial History

JOHN HAYES

ARCO PUBLISHING COMPANY INC.

New York

For
BARBARA
qui sait bien la vie

Published by ARCO PUBLISHING COMPANY, INC.
219 Park Avenue South, New York, NY 10003

First Published in USA 1969

Library of Congress Catalog Number: 69-14963
ARCO Catalog Number: 668-01882-8

Printed and bound in Denmark by F. E. Bording Limited, Copenhagen

Preface

The idea of this book originated with an exhibition called *The Growth of London* which was held at the Victoria and Albert Museum in the summer of 1964. Much careful thought was given to the choice of the exhibits on that occasion, and I make no apology for the fact that many of them, in particular those in the seventeenth and eighteenth century sections for which I was responsible, should re-appear in the illustrations here. Some of the thousands of people who enjoyed the exhibition will perhaps welcome this.

A large number of the illustrations are from paintings, drawings and prints in the London Museum. There are two advantages to this. First, it is the collection with which I am most familiar. Second, it deserves to be better known to a wider public.

J.H.
London, 1968

The Illustrations

Bibliography

The number of books about the development of London is so vast that the only useful kind of bibliography is a short one. The following are among those which have been found by the present writer both indispensable and stimulating:

Nikolaus Pevsner's two volumes on *London* in *The Buildings of England* series, a detailed and personal architectural guide to the surviving fabric of the whole metropolis (Penguin Books 1952 and 1957)

Steen Eiler Rasmussen's brilliant analysis of the development of London from the point of view of town-planning, *London: The Unique City*, 1934 (Penguin Books 1960)

The catalogue of *Printed Maps of London c. 1553–1850* by Ida Darlington and James Howgego (George Philip 1964)

Ralph Merrifield, *The Roman City of London* (Ernest Benn 1965)

Sir Frank Stenton's essay on *Norman London*, which contains a translation of William Fitz Stephen's *Description* and a reconstruction map of London in the reign of Henry II by Marjorie Honeybourne (Historical Association 1934)

Sylvia Thrupp's study of *The Merchant Class of Medieval London* (Ann Arbor Paperbacks 1962)

Stow's *Survey of London*, the text of 1603 edited by C. L. Kingsford (Oxford 1908)

Norman G. Brett-James, *The Growth of Stuart London* (George Allen and Unwin 1935)

T. F. Reddaway, *The Rebuilding of London after the Great Fire* (Jonathan Cape 1940)

Sir John Summerson's classic *Georgian London*, 1945 (Penguin Books 1962)

T. C. Barker and Michael Robbins, *A History of London Transport*, a detailed but broad study which takes the economic and social factors into account: only the first volume on the nineteenth century has so far appeared (George Allen and Unwin 1963)

H. J. Dyos' detailed case-history *Victorian Suburb: A Study of the Growth of Camberwell* (Leicester University Press, 1961)

Greater London, a volume of essays by a group of geographers, edited by J. T. Coppock and H. C. Prince (Faber and Faber 1964)

For those who wish to pursue further any aspect of London's history, there is an invaluable bibliography compiled in 1939 (Greater London Council publication No. 3448)

Introduction

In 1911 Baedeker described London as 'the greatest city in the modern world'. And indeed it must have presented a peerless spectacle to the visitor in those days of Imperial grandeur, commercial supremacy and incomparable social splendour. London in the mid-twentieth century is arguably still the greatest, most lively and most civilised city on earth. For millions of its citizens, as for generations of Londoners before, it offers a way of life uniquely rich and varied. But, physically, it has degenerated. It has reached out too far into the Home Counties, and would continue to do so unchecked had it not been abruptly stopped by statute. Traffic has taken over and obscured the streets. Its fabric has become fragmented: though it is right that the aesthetic heritage of the past should be preserved, the past as such has become an obsession as in no previous age in history, an obvious instance being the frequent reversion to Tudor or Georgian as models for both domestic and public architecture. In too few areas (Poplar, Roehampton, Barbican are among notable exceptions) is there any well-defined twentieth-century character. Or even character at all: whole districts have become a sort of no-man's land, and viewed from afar, from say, the heights of Parliament Hill Fields, London is an amorphous mass of building difficult to distinguish from any other incipient skyscraper city.

But it does remain possible to decipher, between the twentieth-century infilling and papering over and traffic engineering, many layers of London's historical development. The layout of the Mayfair squares remains, though nearly every house has gone. The interminable partially stuccoed terraces of late Georgian London can be visualised at once if one looks down Gloucester Place or Gower Street. The true majesty of the Regent's Street is still revealed, in spite of the almost complete rebuilding, if one drives its length from Pall Mall to the Park on a traffic-free Sunday morning. And the layers of Victorian London lie perhaps too heavy around us: South Kensington Italianate, Baron's Court red brick, debased Gothic in the inner suburbs. Is it possible to reconstruct the way in which these layers came into being and what London actually looked like at any period in its past? And really to appreciate the nature of the city when there were less than a million inhabitants (no further back than the beginning of the last century), or merely 20,000? And where does its history eventually begin?

Effectively, it starts with the invasion of Claudius in AD 43. For though the Thames was a much frequented waterway in prehistoric times, and there were already a number of settlements along its banks, notably between Battersea and Mortlake, there is no archaeological evidence to suggest that settlement had yet begun on the site of London itself. To the Romans, however, this position had particular advantages. It was essential for them to bridge the Thames if communications were to be maintained in the south-east of Britain, and they also required a port. The site of London was the point nearest to the estuary where the river was still tidal (and therefore navigable) that it was possible to build a bridge: the southern shore was least marshy here, and on the north bank the physical conditions were ideal, as hard, well-drained gravel soil extended down to the river itself. Also, the land on the north bank rose to well-defined hills in two places, with streams on either side, and these provided naturally defensible positions of an elementary sort.

The Roman bridge (or bridges, as there were no doubt several replacements over the centuries) was constructed a little to the east of the present London Bridge, and settlement started at the bridgehead, on the eastern of the two hills (Cornhill). Not that growth was haphazard, as has usually been maintained: the road system was almost certainly planned, as was customary in any Roman town, and part of an east-west Roman road dating from this early period lies beneath modern Lombard Street; in all probability, though there is no evidence to prove it, the great arterial roads fanning out to Silchester, Verulamium (St Albans) and Camulodunum (Colchester), the capital of the province, were part of the original street plan. A modest basilica (town-hall) was built, but there were few other buildings of

importance, and, though the clay soil around London provided excellent material for brick-making, most of the houses were simple dwellings of wattle and daub construction. By mid-century, settlement was beginning on the western hill, and Tacitus reported that the city was fast becoming a prosperous trading community.

Then, almost without warning, came total annihilation. In the year AD 61, when Suetonius Paulinus, the military governor, was campaigning in Wales, the tribesmen of East Anglia, enraged by the petty spitefulness of local officialdom, rose up in revolt and took a terrible revenge: their army, headed by Queen Boudicca of the Iceni, sacked and burnt in quick succession the towns of Camulodunum, Verulamium and London.

London, rebuilt after the sack, replaced Colchester as the Roman capital, and rapidly became a city of considerable importance. The whole town was now replanned; the new basilica was vast, some 500 feet long, one of the largest in the Empire; expansion took place

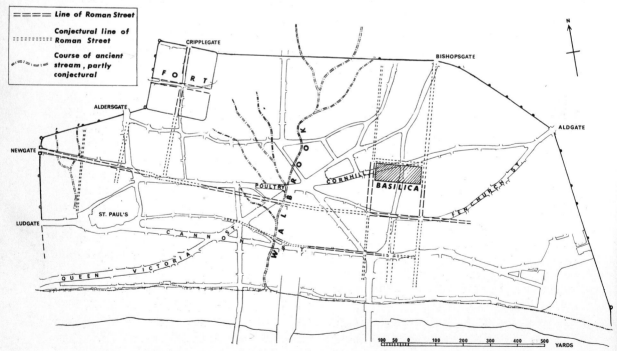

Sketch map of Roman London showing the relationship of the Roman road system to the present streets.

both to the east and to the north, though the existence of cemeteries in the area later occupied by St Paul's shows that settlement had not reached very far westwards (burial was not permitted within the confines of a Roman town); and to the north-west of the town, some little way out, a large stone fort was built (the Cripplegate fort), evidently less a defensive structure than the headquarters for the kind of permanent garrison normally attached to a Roman capital city.

London was once again destroyed by fire in about AD 125–30, and once again rebuilt. In the late second century, the marshy area between the two hills, where up to then a market had flourished along the banks of the Walbrook, was reclaimed and became a smart residential district; the important Mithraic temple excavated in 1954 served this neighbourhood. And also at this period, or perhaps later (the evidence is unclear), a defensive wall was built round London; contrary to general supposition, this seems not to have been completed along the riverfront. London never grew outside its walls in Roman times, and settlement was fairly sparse even in certain areas within. The population, though impossible to calculate now, was never large; the huts and shacks of the poor may have grown up close to larger houses and public buildings, but there was no serious overcrowding.

In the course of the third century, troubles on the Continent in the shape of barbarian invasion and civil war brought disaster to London's overseas trade, and the fortunes of the city must gradually have collapsed; fine new houses were still being put up quite late in the century, but it is disquieting evidence that it was permissible to take building materials from deserted temples. Then, in the early fourth century, came the first of the Saxon invasions, and, finally, in AD 410, when Italy itself was being ravaged by the Goths, Britain was abandoned by the Romans, and the Saxons had a free hand.

Records are scanty for the Saxon period, but there is no reason to believe that London was then deserted for a century and more—indeed we know that in AD 457 the Britons fled from Kent to the protection of the city; but it declined into a purely local community. It may well have maintained its population and its crafts, but not its status, its government, its civic buildings, or its trade. Saxon communities settled nearby, along the banks of the Thames, the closest settlement being in the vicinity of where the Savoy Hotel now stands, but being primarily a farming people, they did not occupy the city itself for some considerable time.

It can be established however that by the beginning of the seventh century London was the chief town of the East Saxons; and the Kentish kings, overlords of the East Saxons, who had been converted to Christianity by St Augustine, set up bishoprics in Rochester and London in AD 604. A church was built on the highest ground in the city, and was dedicated to St Paul; active settlement now began around St Paul's, and development spread gradually eastwards, thus following the opposite course to the expansion of the Roman city. The foundation of All Hallows, Barking, in the third quarter of the seventh century, indicates that development had already reached this area. Of the street plan of Saxon London nothing certain is known, though it may be inferred that at any rate the principal streets of the medieval city followed an earlier pre-Conquest pattern.

In the second quarter of the eighth century London came under the overlordship of the Mercian kings, and there are references to their control of the port; according to Bede, the city was now enjoying a renewed commercial prosperity and was trading extensively with the continent. Something of its European importance is suggested by Bishop Helmstan of Winchester, who wrote in AD 839 that he had been consecrated 'in the illustrious place, built by the skill of the ancient Romans, called throughout the world the great city of London'.

The city was well organised defensively and held out vigorously against the continued attacks of first the Vikings and then the Danes, becoming the centre of national resistance in this dark period of British history. In AD 886 the walls were strengthened by King Alfred, great bastions were built in appropriate positions along their length, and the bridge was protected with parapets and towers; ten years later, we hear of Alfred camping close to London so that the citizens could reap their corn in safety in the fields outside the city. Twice however, once in the ninth century and again in AD 982, the defences failed and the city was sacked by the Danes; finally in AD 1016 a compact was made between Edmund Ironside and Cnut by which the latter was allotted the whole of England beyond the Thames, and London had perforce to settle with the Danes.

Though much of London was composed of simple timber-framed huts, so that fires must still have been frequent (St Paul's burnt down in AD 961), by the eleventh century it was recognised as the foremost city in the country. Foreign trade was continually expanding, and among specific instances the Church of St Peter of Ghent is known to have had a special wharf, while the men of Rouen are recorded as coming to the wharves of Dowgate with wine and the larger sorts of fish. More significant than commercial wealth, when the succession to the throne was in dispute in AD 1042 it was at London that Edward the Confessor was elected king by popular acclamation.

The court was now more frequently near London than at Winchester (Cnut had his palace at Westminster, on Thorney Island) and it was the development there in later centuries of the institutions of national government that finally assured the greatness of the city. The Confessor began building his great abbey (Westminster) on a site formerly occupied by a monastery, and the remains of a Saxon hall excavated in Whitehall indicates that there was other settlement in this area. Westminster may already have been a small town.

From what is known of London's government at this time, its institutions were entirely Saxon; it is a significant fact that there is nothing to suggest continuity with the Roman system of administration. The most important institution was the folk-moot, which met three times a year on the open ground north-east of St Paul's, and was attended by every citizen. Civil and commercial disputes were settled in the husting, which met once a week, and where a body of aldermen sat apart as a bench of persons learned in the law. These same aldermen presided over lesser courts in each of the wards into which the city was by now divided. There is also evidence that London administered wide areas of the countryside surrounding.

When William the Conqueror finally received the submission of London after his victory over Harold at Hastings in 1066, he retained a healthy respect for the political maturity and potential military capacity of the city. He was careful at his coronation to ask the assembled people if they accepted him as their lord, careful also to guarantee the rights and privileges of the citizens: 'I will that ye be all those laws worthy, that ye were in King Edward's day.' In addition, he built a castle to the east of the city as an earnest of his own military strength, and 'against the fickleness of the vast and fierce populace'; this was later replaced by the mighty hall-keep known as the White Tower.

The ward, which had responsibility for defence and keeping watch, continued to be the unit of London's government in Norman times, and, not unexpectedly, it was the aldermen who emerged as the leaders of the city. The power of London now increased rapidly; the citizens were known collectively as barons, and they took advantage of political dissensions at court to further civic autonomy—financial and political assistance were offered to the Crown in return for specific privileges. The celebrated charter which was granted to London by Henry I between 1130 and 1133 mainly confirmed existing privileges, such as the citizens' hunting rights in Surrey, Middlesex and the Chilterns, but it also surrendered the right of appointing a sheriff, a right that can hardly be over-estimated, since the sheriff was primarily a royal official, and responsible for the collection and return of royal revenue.

During the troubled years that followed, the citizens acted as a corporate body, and they were recognised as such by factions outside. It was this experience of corporate action that led to the establishment of the commune in 1191, and the extraction from King John of the right to elect a Mayor—a milestone in London's history.

The population at this date was probably in the region of 20,000, and except along the riverfront (where a new London Bridge of stone had been begun in 1176) and in the vicinity of Cheap, London was no more densely settled than in Roman times, and 'blest in the wholesomeness of its air'. Almost all the Norman magnates owned mansions there, 'lordly habitations ... whither they repair and wherein they make lavish outlay, when summoned to the City by our Lord the King'. Some leading citizens possessed houses that were surrounded by defensible walls (these were the burhs familiar from names like Lothbury), and a frontage of 30–40 feet may have been normal. Many houses within the walls had gardens, even orchards, though there is no evidence that agriculture was carried on; animals, expecially pigs, were kept in abundance but were apt to stray and become a nuisance: among the several ordinances on this subject is one of 1277–8 enjoining that 'no pig be henceforth found by the streets or lanes of the City or suburb'.

William Fitz Stephen, the earliest medieval chronicler to write a description of the city, took special delight in its environs: 'On all sides, beyond the houses, lie the gardens of the citizens that dwell in the suburbs, planted with trees, spacious and fair, adjoining one another. On the north are pasture lands and a pleasant space of flat meadows. ... There are also round about London in the Suburbs most excellent wells, whose waters are sweet, wholesome and clear.' At Westminster, which became the favoured residence of the Norman kings, 'the Royal Palace rises high above the river ... two miles from the City and joined thereto by a populous suburb'.

London was noted for 'its reverence for the Christian faith', and there were well over a hundred parish churches. St Paul's already had its school. Most of the sokes or liberties that abounded were ecclesiastical. The oldest monastery was St Martin-le-Grand, founded before 1068; many others were instituted in the twelfth century, including those of the Knights Templars, and the foundations of the friars followed in the thirteenth.

In Henry III's reign London finally became the permanent political and administrative capital of the nation, and during the course of the thirteenth century the population increased rapidly; at its end the city was overflowing beyond the walls, notably on the west side, and this westerly drift (from now on the characteristic of fashionable growth) was accentuated in the fourteenth century by the establishment of the Inns of Court in a belt northwards from the Temple. Well over a third of London's inhabitants died from the fearsome ravages of the Black Death, but by 1377, a quarter of a century later, the evidence points to a population of about 40,000, a figure more than three times that of medieval York or Bristol, and comparable to the wealthy burgher cities of the Low Countries, Bruges, Ghent and Brussels. Many of the new immigrants (who were known as 'foreigners', to distinguish them from the citizens or freemen on the one hand and aliens on the other) arrived from the home counties, but many came from the eastern shires and from the north of England.

London was fast becoming the cramped and crowded city familiar to us from Stow's account two centuries later. All waste sites had been developed, the Walbrook was covered over, the area round Cheap was a rabbit-warren of tenements and alleys, 50 steep lanes sloped down to the river (which was lined with warehouses), and houses encroached onto London Bridge. By 1381 there were three new parishes, the ward of Farringdon Without was created in 1393 to administer the western suburbs, and the beginnings of an 'east end' are discernible, for it was poorer people who tended to settle in Portsoken or Bishopsgate. Southwark was already noted for harbouring

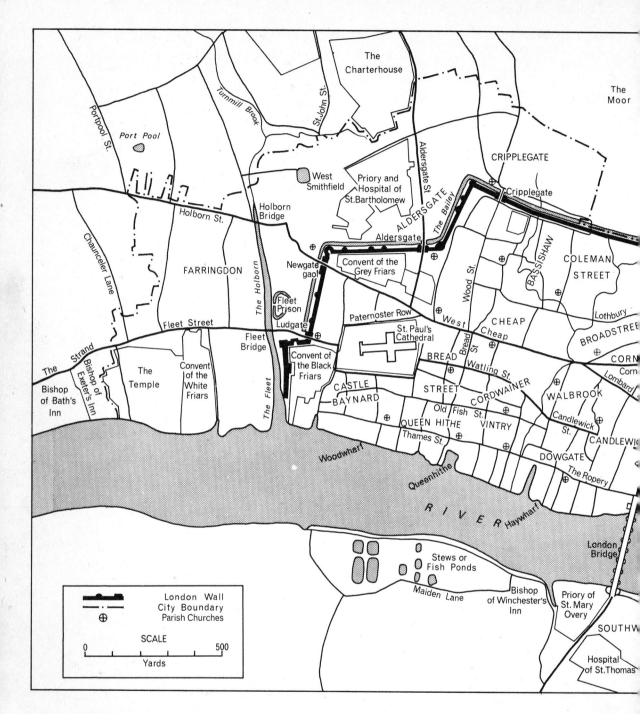

The Charterhouse

The Moor

CRIPPLEGATE

Cripplegate

Portpool St.

Port Pool

Turnmill Brook

St. John St.

Aldersgate St.

West Smithfield

Priory and Hospital of St. Bartholomew

ALDERSGATE

The Bailey

BASSISHAW

COLEMAN STREET

Chaunceler Lane

Holborn St.

Holborn Bridge

Aldersgate

Newgate gaol

Convent of the Grey Friars

Wood St.

CHEAP

FARRINGDON

The Holborn

Fleet Prison

Ludgate

Paternoster Row

St. Paul's Cathedral

West Cheap

Lothbury

BROADSTREE

Fleet Street

Fleet Bridge

The Fleet

BREAD

Bread St.

Watling St.

STREET

CORDWAINER

CORN

Corn

Lombard

The Strand

Bishop of Exeter's Inn

The Temple

Convent of the White Friars

Convent of the Black Friars

CASTLE BAYNARD

Old Fish St.

VINTRY

WALBROOK

Candlewick St.

CANDLEWIC

Bishop of Bath's Inn

QUEEN HITHE

Thames St.

DOWGATE

The Ropery

Woodwharf

Queenhithe

Haywharf

R I V E R

London Bridge

Stews or Fish Ponds

London Bridge

Maiden Lane

Bishop of Winchester's Inn

Priory of St. Mary Overy

SOUTHW

Hospital of St. Thomas

London Wall
City Boundary
⊕   Parish Churches

SCALE

0   500

Yards

Sketch map of London in the later Middle Ages
showing the crowded riverfront, the palaces of the
bishops along the Strand, and the extent to which the
land around the city was owned by monastic foundations. Five wards without the walls are marked.

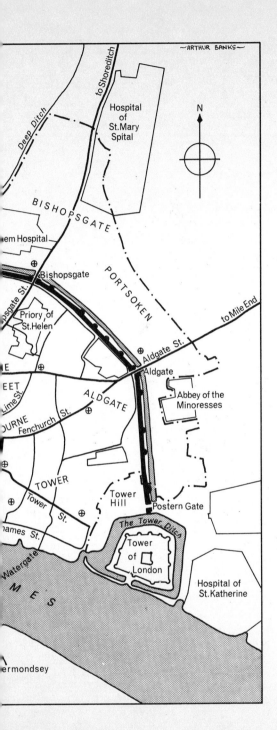

felons and for its 'stews', the red-light district of medieval London; but though it was described as virtually a second town, it was not incorporated into the city until the creation of the ward of Bridge Without in 1550.

The congestion of London in the later Middle Ages may be guessed at from the definition of a street as a thoroughfare sufficiently broad for a couple of loaded carts to pass each other by, whereas a lane was often only negotiable on horseback or on foot, and could be as narrow as five feet. It is small wonder that the air in the heart of London became increasingly unhealthy. The city ditches were often full of filth and dunghills, the streets a common receptacle for refuse, and infection and disease spread easily.

The main highway for all forms of traffic was the Thames, and it remained so until the eighteenth century. The broadest street was West Cheap, which was really an extended market square, and the centre of most commercial activity; on both sides of it, appropriately, were streets named after commodities, Bread Street, Milk Street, the Poultry. Other streets were named after occupations, Cordwainer Street, for instance, or Ironmonger Lane; Stinking Lane was in the butchers' quarter. West Cheap, where the goldsmiths had their shops, was known simply as 'the street'; it was also the place where tournaments were held. The names East and West Cheap (and East and West Smithfield) recalled the origins of London on the two hills on either side of the Walbrook.

Fitz Stephen said that 'the only plagues of London are the immoderate drinking of fools and the frequency of fires'. There was a considerable amount of violence, too, which often developed into riot. But fire was a particular menace to life and property, for despite innumerable ordinances which decreed the replacement of wood by stone, and thatch by tile, houses continued to be built of timber and plaster. Overhanging upper storeys were common, so urgent was the need for space, and for most people living quarters were unbelievably confined; craftsmen lived above their shops, the poor were crowded into tenements and the extent of their poverty is underlined by the constant melancholy refrain in the coroners' rolls: 'Chattels and goods had he none'.

Yet in this period London was also a city of considerable and even widespread wealth, ostentatiously so by the fifteenth century, when it was handling the greater part of the English wool trade. Many foreign businessmen found it profitable to live there; Danish and Norwegian traders had possessed this right since Norman times, Italians gave their name to Lombard Street, and the Hanseatic merchants occupied a walled precinct on the riverfront near Dowgate, the famous Steelyard.

This was the golden age of the gilds. Some craft gilds, such as the weavers, the fishmongers and the bakers, were in existence as early as the twelfth century; by the end of Edward III's reign in 1377 there were at least 50, by 1400 more than 100. To many of them the Crown had granted Charters of Incorporation, and political power soon followed economic. The gilds controlled conditions of employment and apprenticeship, and the quality of goods produced; it was obviously easier to supervise standards and prevent frauds if members of a particular craft were congregated together, and the occupational nature of certain streets was largely the result of gild ordinances. But they were also delegated the power to settle minor trade disputes. The authority of six gildsmen was the requisite for admitting a 'foreigner' to the freedom of the City. The more important gildsmen were allowed the privilege of wearing a distinctive dress, and were known as liverymen. And the gilds eventually acquired the right of electing the Mayor and Sheriffs, though the Common Council continued to be chosen by the wards.

Map of Elizabethan London showing the growth outside the walls, notably to the north-west of the city, and in ribbon development along Bishopsgate and towards Mile End. Westminster, once a separate town, is connected to London via the Strand, but St Giles is still in the fields.

Participation in the city's administrative affairs, the building of Guildhall, and the emergence of the 12 great Companies, were all symptomatic of where real power now lay. In the fifteenth century London was an oligarchy, ruled by its wealthiest merchant class, the 'merchauntis full of substaunce and of myght' of Dunbar's poem. These patricians built great houses for themselves, usually planned as 'inns', with entrance gatehouse, a grand hall and of course warehouses. They dressed sumptuously in rich furs, and impressed visitors with their collections of gold and silver plate: even a Venetian was amazed by the sight of 52 goldsmiths in a single street. At the end of the Middle Ages, London was already a city of stark contrasts.

This contrast between fantastic wealth and

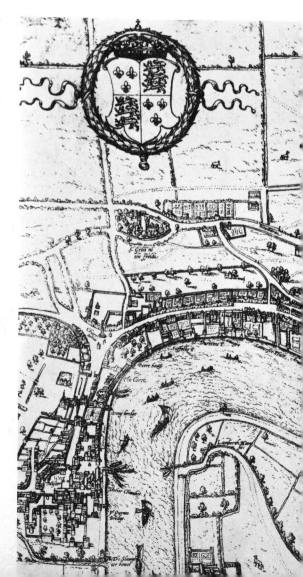

bitter poverty was further accentuated during the century of Tudor rule, and especially in Elizabeth's reign. Cloth exports doubled under Henry VIII, and by 1558, largely due to the judicious advice of Sir Thomas Gresham, economic adviser to the Crown, London had replaced Antwerp as the financial centre of northern Europe; the Hanseatic merchants were deprived of their special privileges, loans were no longer floated abroad, and the City became the source of mercantile credit and the underwriter of government. The first joint-stock company, the Muscovy Company, was founded in 1555, and others, notably the great East India Company, followed. New industries developed in London, of which glass making was one. Expeditions all over the world were either London-based or London-financed.

And the splendid visual symbol of this shift of financial power was the Royal Exchange, planned by Gresham and completed in 1569.

But, at the same time and for the same reasons, the conditions of life in the metropolis were worsening. Increasing rural unemployment due to the enclosure of agricultural land for sheep-farming coincided with the commercial boom in London. Attracted by the boundless opportunities which seemed to be offered by the capital, immigrants poured in from the provinces. The population rose dramatically. Still about 40,000 in 1485, and no more than 50,000 by 1530, it had increased to well over 200,000 by the end of the sixteenth century. Five times as many people were now living in London. Where did these newcomers find a home? What indeed could most of them

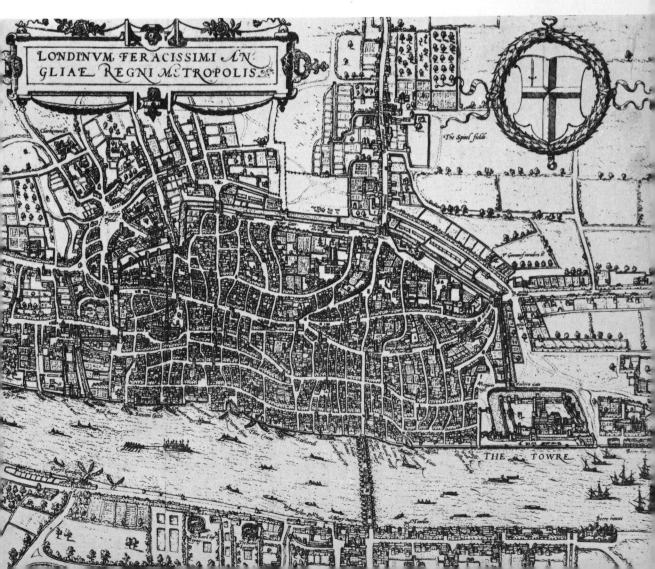

afford in a period of continually and sharply rising prices?

A great deal of valuable land within the city was freed for building purposes when the monastic estates were confiscated by Henry VIII; and many former religious buildings were simply converted into tenements. But more of the newcomers were accommodated without the walls than within them, and ribbon development soon stretched out far to the north, while substantial and appallingly overcrowded suburbs grew up to the west of the city, round Smithfield and towards Holborn, and to the east, in the direction of Mile End and Stepney. Stow described the road beyond Bishopsgate as 'all along a continuall building of small and base tenements, for the most part lately erected', and the highway from Wapping to Radcliffe as even worse, 'a continuall streete, or filthy straight passage, with Alleyes of small tenements or cottages builded'.

The overcrowding and lack of sanitation resulted in increasingly severe outbreaks of bubonic plague, and the problem of the 'sinfully-polluted suburbes', which lay outside the jurisdiction of the City and gilds, began to alarm the government (some of the worst slums were growing up round Westminster). Beggars and vagrants were required to return to their places of origin, and in 1580 the first of a series of royal proclamations on London housing recommended that no more than a single family should occupy one house, and that no new buildings should be constructed within three miles of the City gates; this was reinforced by statute in 1593, but in spite of the fines imposed, the effect was slight. The law was difficult to enforce (as always with legislation in restraint of slums), and simply encouraged the growth of shanties, temporary structures which took permanent root; it also encouraged yet more building inside the walls, mainly additions to existing houses, though 'middle rows' were developed in certain streets.

The houses of the great still stood along the waterfront of the Strand, from the Temple to Charing Cross, and many were added or rebuilt at this time; the grandest of the new mansions were Somerset House, built at the end of the 1540s by the Lord Protector, and Northumberland House, begun at the very close of the Tudor period by Elizabeth's first minister, Robert Cecil (this survived until 1874). In 1551 the Venetian ambassador remarked on the 'many large palaces making a fine show', but also how London was 'disfigured by the ruins of a multitude of churches and monasteries'. Some of the latter, such as the Charterhouse, were converted into schools, and other schools (Merchant Taylors' is an example) were founded by the livery companies or by wealthy merchants to replace the monastic foundations; unlike most capital cities, London had never possessed a university, and Gresham endowed a college in his house in Broad Street which was intended to supply this need.

It was James I's ambition to be able to say that he 'had found our Citie and suburbs of London of stickes, and left them of bricke, being a material farre more durable, safe from fire and beautiful and magnificent'. Brick had already begun to be used extensively as a building material in place of wood (which was required for ship-building) in Elizabethan times, and during the 1570s Spitalfield, part of the estate of a dissolved priory that had become a recreation ground, was 'broken up for clay to make brick'. Covent Garden, laid out during the 1630s, was built entirely of brick. It was also the earliest example of planned domestic building in London, and the first regular piece of street development since the Romans.

The laws in restraint of building now compelled developers to seek a licence from the Crown, and Charles I, who dreamt of a capital city that would enhance the glory of the Stuart monarchy, could require those to whom licences were granted to build in a manner that conformed to his ideas of the new Renaissance London. So when the Earl of Bedford sought to develop Covent Garden, for profit, Inigo Jones was installed as supervising architect, and a splendid square of houses of uniform type, no doubt inspired by his memories of the Place des Vosges in Paris, was planned. A slightly later development of a similar sort was begun in 1638 in Lincoln's Inn Fields. Jones, who had earlier built the Banqueting House subsequently decorated by Rubens, also prepared numerous drawings for a magnificent new palace of Whitehall for Charles I, but this scheme came to nothing: the Crown lacked sufficient funds, and eventually the Civil War intervened.

London, the merchant city, was a staunch supporter of the Parliamentary cause; defence works consisting of 24 forts and 18 miles of trenches were constructed by the citizens when the Royalists threatened London, and the trained bands of the city wards formed a valuable element in Cromwell's army. But the inevitable decline of trade brought hard times to craftsmen and shopkeepers alike, and Lithgow commented in 1643 that he 'never saw *London* these fourtie years past so populous as now it is: only there is a general muttering that money is hard to come by, and that is, because all kinde of trades and trading begin to decay.' The Puritan attitude towards pleasure, the closing of the theatres and similar deprivations, made life even more intolerable.

The Restoration of Charles II was a relief to the citizens in every way, but at the very beginning of this new epoch there occurred disasters on an unprecedented scale. First came an outbreak of the plague ten times more terrible than the visitations of 1625 and 1636. It started in the autumn of 1664 in the slums of St Giles-in-the-Fields, and throughout the long hot summer of 1665 ravaged the whole of London, finally reaching the east end in August and September; in all, about 100,000 people perished. In 1666 it was the turn of that other continual scourge of London—fire. An apparently minor outbreak which started in Pudding Lane, near London Bridge, was somehow allowed to get out of hand, and, fanned by a strong east wind, raged among the timber-built houses of the ancient city for four whole days, leaving four-fifths of the area within the walls in total ruin.

Almost before the ashes had settled, a complete survey of the devastated area was undertaken, and rebuilding began early in 1667. For practical reasons to do with the ownership of land, the various suggestions submitted to the King for simplifying and modernising the layout of the City as a whole were rejected, and, in the main, the former street plan was carefully followed. Certain streets were widened, especially the narrower lanes, and plans were approved for two new thoroughfares, King Street and Queen Street, which ran from Guildhall to the Thames; the congested waterfront between the Bridge and the Tower, which had replaced the downstream quays such as Dowgate and Queenhithe in importance in the Tudor period, was also replanned, and a long stretch of wide embanked quays constructed in its place.

New regulations were rigorously enforced in the rebuilding. Timber construction was at last forbidden, and houses had to be of either brick or stone, with walls of specified thickness. In the principal thoroughfares a building height of four storeys was the rule, in the 'streets and lanes of note' it was three, and in the by-lanes two. It is a tribute to the astonishing resilience of the City of London that all the secular buildings, including the halls of the livery companies, were rebuilt in brick in just five years; the churches took rather longer, though these were finished, too, with the exception of some of their towers and of St Paul's Cathedral itself, by 1686.

But not all the houses were occupied. In 1673 nearly 3,500 remained empty. The disasters of plague and fire, together with the growing impurity of the air in the City, the result of the 'Hellish and dismall Cloud of SEA COAL' produced by '*Brewers, Diers, Sope and Salt-boylers, Lime-burners, and the Like*', had accelerated the tendency among the well-to-do to move westwards into the outskirts of the metropolis. Fine new squares had already been started in Holborn (Bloomsbury Square) and close to St James's Palace, the latter becoming the centre of an elegant new court suburb; landowners were now following the example of Covent Garden of their own

Map of London at the beginning of the Hanoverian period showing the shift of population westwards, and the planning of the early West End squares. Spitalfields has been settled by Huguenot refugees, and poorer development is stretching along the river-front towards Wapping.

accord so as to attract the nobility and a wealthier class of tenant, and the square remained the focal point of London estate development for the next 200 years.

The north side of Piccadilly now became the fashionable place for the mansions of the aristocracy, Burlington House, Berkeley House and others; on the site of Clarendon House, pulled down in 1683, Bond Street and Albemarle Street were built up with houses soon 'inhabited by persons of Quality'. Many of the palaces along the Strand were abandoned as being too close to the City, and speculators, of whom Nicholas Barbon was the most celebrated, ran up streets of houses in their place: part of his Buckingham Street still survives. The City naturally deplored this westward development, and complained in 1675 that the conversion of Essex House 'if permitted will tend to the ruine of said Citty already languishing under great decay of their Retayle Trade'. The house was nevertheless demolished and Essex Street finished by 1682. Barbon was also active in Westminster and Soho, and, in order to protect his property, operated his own up-to-date fire-engines and pioneered house insurance. Other development in these districts was of a meaner sort, and a royal proclamation of 1671 restricting building in the suburbs condemned it for 'Choaking up the Aire of His Majesties Palaces'.

Hackney was still a favoured retreat, noted for its 'healthful air', but Clerkenwell, which had also been a smart residential quarter (Isaak Walton lived on the Green for seventeen years), degenerated into slums in the last quarter of the century. Many of the poorer immigrants to London tended to settle to the

east of the City and the Huguenot refugees, for instance, who developed London's silk industry, congregated in Spitalfields. But the expansion of East London at this period took place mainly along the riverfront, towards Limehouse and Blackwall, and was due to the increasing trade and traffic of the port.

During the course of the seventeenth century, and in spite of the Plague, the population almost trebled, from close on 250,000 to very nearly 750,000. Sir William Petty, the distinguished economist, who believed that London would re-double its population every 40 years, calculated that 'the Growth of London must stop of its self, before the Year 1800'. Another writer, Fletcher, anticipated the

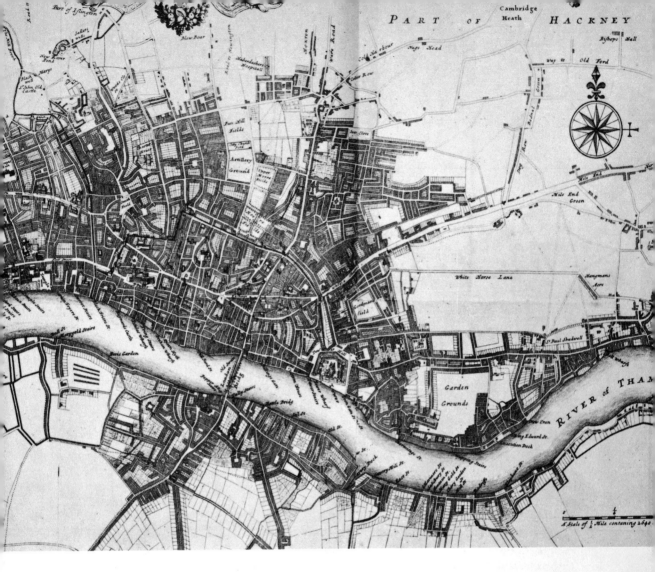

decentralisation policies of the mid-twentieth century when he suggested in 1703 that the country would be better off with 12 great cities 'possessed of equal advantages'.

In the event, Petty was quite wrong. London's population did not increase substantially during the eighteenth century. When the first Census was taken in 1801, it stood at a little over 950,000; poverty, disease and the consumption of cheap spirits were responsible for a particularly high death rate in the first half of the century. But the extent of London did increase, considerably, and notably in the West End. Cavendish and Hanover Squares were the centre of the earliest development; Grosvenor and Berkeley Squares followed,

and by mid-century most of the present Mayfair had been laid out with spacious streets of fine brick houses. The Portman estate, north of the Oxford Road, was developed after 1760, and the pace of building in the West End did not slacken until the beginning of the wars with France in the 1790s.

By the end of the eighteenth century Oxford Street had replaced Cheapside, and to a certain extent also the Strand, as the finest shopping street in the metropolis. Markets now flourished in the West End (Covent Garden had been authorised in 1669, Hungerford in 1678) and tradespeople and craftsmen had also moved there long since, continuing a process which had begun in the sixteenth century; the economic monopolies of the City, and the power of the gilds, were in evident decline.

What was lacking outside the City however was any effective system of local government. Charles I had tried to establish a separate Corporation for the suburbs (it was one of the reasons why the City opposed him in the Civil War), but the experiment was unsuccessful. Up to the middle of the nineteenth century these overpopulated and often turbulent parts of London were nominally governed by the unpaid officers of the parish—authorities who might still do well enough in a country village but had neither the energy nor the funds to deal with urban problems. Hospitals and schools continued to be founded by private benefaction; the West End squares set up their own trustees to pave, cleanse and light their streets; turnpike trusts authorised by Parliament maintained the main roads in return for the right to exact tolls; and commissioners were appointed for particular improvements, such as the building of Westminster Bridge.

Westminster and Blackfriars Bridges, with their fine approach roads, opened up the marshy area of St George's Fields; St George's Circus was laid out in 1769, and in the 1780s streets of houses began to link up the ancient borough of Southwark with Lambeth, though development did not begin in earnest until the end of the Napoleonic Wars. To the north of London, a by-pass was constructed, the New Road from Paddington to the City, and by the end of the century, development in the shape of 'new towns' had started beyond this artery, first Pentonville, then Somers Town and Camden Town. Much of the work here was inferior to contemporary development in Bloomsbury, which had begun in about 1775 with Bedford Square, and in 1810 Nash complained that 'houses of such a mean sort as have been built at Somers Town, and are now building on Lord Southampton's ground, should disgrace this apex of the Metropolis'.

The truth is that the demand for housing was rapidly beginning to outrun supply, since

in the short period between 1801 and 1841 London's population doubled, from under a million to nearly two millions. About a third of the immigrants settled in the poorer eastern suburbs, creating a belt of slums which stretched from Finsbury to Bermondsey, and though seriously disturbing both the health and the conscience of the Victorian city, not yet entirely eradicated.

This startling rise in population, fulfilling Petty's fears and forecast, was due to one over-riding cause, the Industrial Revolution. The collapse of a settled agrarian economy, and the opportunities for employment (however miserable) in the factories and mills, had brought countrymen into the towns by tens of thousands. London was not only the largest manufacturing centre of all (predominating, for instance, in shipbuilding throughout the nineteenth century), but the focal point of the distributing trades; these now enjoyed an ever-increasing prosperity and no wealthy Victorian merchant or industrialist but had an office in London.

The volume of imports and exports handled by the port was already so great in the last decade of the eighteenth century that to accommodate the shipping a vast new system of docks was constructed between 1800 and 1830. Internal communications were also improved. The Commercial Road was formed to connect the City and the docks. Regent's Canal was cut to extend the Grand Union Canal (which linked London with the Midlands) to the Thames at Limehouse, between the new London and West India docks. Great trunk roads, of which the most important was the Finchley Road, were built northwards from the New Road, by-passing the hills of Hampstead and Highgate so as to afford easy gradients for heavy waggons. And the new fast mail-coach services provided frequent passenger connections to all parts of Britain.

In the metropolis itself, northward expansion was inhibited by the difficulty of travelling to Westminster through the unplanned streets of Soho and Holborn (largely late seventeenth-century slums) until Nash built Regent Street, carefully aligned so as to provide 'a boundary and complete separation between the Streets and Squares occupied by the Nobility and Gentry, and the narrow Streets and meaner Houses occupied by mechanics and the trading part of the community'. The development of St John's Wood with terraces and villas followed hard on the layout of Regent's Park. Building also began in Bayswater, but the most spectacular extension of the Nash style occurred in the marshes of the Five Fields, beyond Westminster: it was Thomas Cubitt, London's most enterprising builder since Barbon, who drained the land, made use of the earth which had been excavated for the construction of St Katharine's Dock, and built the imposing squares and streets of Belgravia (and later, Pimlico).

The even more phenomenal expansion of London which took place in the Victorian age (the population then increased from under two millions to something like six-and-a-half) was due entirely to vastly improved transport facilities; and the history of the metropolis since 1837 has followed a broadly similar pattern, a sequence of improvements in communications, outward expansion, increasing population, and congestion at the centre, repeated over and over again.

The first new means of transport was the omnibus, which became ubiquitous in the 1840s and 1850s (the London General Omnibus Company was formed in 1855) and successfully withstood competition from the early railways, for the simple reason that it took the passenger right to his destination; the only early railway termini close to the heart of the City were Liverpool Street, Fenchurch Street and London Bridge. But travelling was not so cheap that everyone could afford to use either trains or 'buses. A high percentage of the population still lived close to their places of work; and in 1854 it was estimated that 200,000 people came into the City every day on foot, from suburbs as far off as Peckham or Camberwell.

The traffic congestion caused by the increasing number of 'bus services was eased by

certain street improvements (New Oxford Street was formed in 1845–7 to connect Oxford Street with Holborn); but more significant were the extension of the southern railways to termini north of the river, to Victoria, Charing Cross, and Cannon Street, and the creation of the underground. From the 1860s a complex network of railways began to enmesh London, and flourishing new suburbs like Sydenham and Croydon grew up round the stations. The resident population of the City declined sharply as a house in the outer parts of London—a constant dream among the well-to-do since Tudor times at least—was made possible for a much wider class of people not only by a general increase in prosperity in the last quarter of the nineteenth century (a period of rising incomes and falling prices), but by the introduction of cheap fares for working men: in 1874 Tunbridge Wells actually petitioned Parliament against cheaper fares as an influence likely to lower the social tone of the town. Suburban growth was perhaps most rapid in the north, in districts such as Edmonton and Walthamstow, which were also served by trams, while as far out as Finchley the population doubled in this period.

With the building of the great new railway termini, many slums, in Somers Town, Agar Town and elsewhere, were cleared, but others soon grew up, and the inner suburbs close to the City all harboured notorious rookeries. In St Giles in 1836 there were instances of 15 people sharing a single room, 'in one corner of the room, lodgers, in another corner another set of lodgers, and besides a separate set of lodgers in the centre of the room, all distinct'. Cholera, a disease imported from the East, began to ravage London in the 1840s and scared government into legislation on public health. Prince Albert was among the pioneers of model houses for the working classes, and in the 1860s numerous rather grim-looking blocks of tenements were constructed in the poorer parts of inner London under the aegis of Baroness Burdett-Coutts and by the Peabody Trust. Open spaces were among other amenities planned; Victoria Park, over 200 acres in extent, was laid out in the 1840s, and Battersea Park was opened in 1853. Slum clearance was combined with the relief of traffic congestion in planning street improvements, and Victoria Street was driven through the worst of Westminster's slums in the 1850s.

Most important of all, there was at last created, in 1856, an administrative body for the whole of London outside the City, the Metropolitan Board of Works, which was charged particularly with 'the better management of the metropolis in respect of the sewerage and drainage and the paving, cleansing, lighting and improvements thereof'. A comprehensive new sewage system was constructed with outfalls well below the City, the unhealthy river front was embanked from Westminster to Blackfriars, and slum clearance was continued, one of the Board's last schemes being the construction in the 1880s of Shaftesbury Avenue and Charing Cross Road.

When the County Councils Act was passed in 1888, London was made a county, and the new authority assumed the responsibilities of the Metropolitan Board of Works. It was ironic, however, that scarcely had the boundaries of the new county been defined than they were outstripped by suburban growth. Nor were the powers of the London County Council complete. The City had not been included in the new authority, and remained defiantly independent; and when the archaic system of parish administration was finally swept away in 1899, it was replaced by 28 autonomous boroughs, each with its Mayor and Aldermen—'there was to be not one London but thirty Birminghams'. As if this complexity was not enough, there were other independent bodies, the London School Board (taken over by the Council in 1904), and the Port of London Authority, set up in 1909, the first task of which was to save London as a trading centre by cutting a channel in the river sufficiently deep for the draught of modern shipping.

London at the beginning of the present century was a city of divided authority, sprawling unplanned suburbs, congested streets, smoke, fogs and grime. It was also

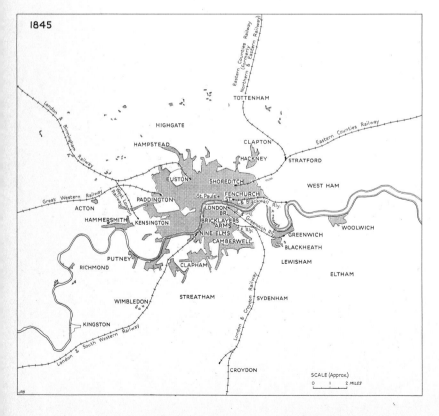

Sketch map of London at the beginning Queen Victoria's reign marking the earlie railways and their metropolitan termini.

the richest city in the world, with a volume of trade ten times greater than in 1800, its opulence and sense of grandeur symbolised by such improvements as Kingsway and the Mall. The atmosphere was one of serene self-confidence. The coming of the motor vehicle was thought for a time to have ended traffic blocks for ever. Experiments in garden city layout, of which Hampstead Garden Suburb was the chief, were regarded as the solution to the problem of the dreary and interminable suburban streets. Then came the disillusion of the First World War, and with it the end of an age of optimism and economic expansion.

Following the war, an abortive attempt was made by the Ullswater Commission of 1921 to reform London's hopelessly contradictory system of government. Its failure was probably the greatest single cause of the continued disintegration of the metropolis. The London County Council resumed its pre-war programmes of slum clearance and housing, but it failed to create a new township out of its most ambitous scheme, the Becontree–Dagenham estate, largely because of adminis-trative confusion: the estate lay not only outside the county, in Essex, but in three different local authority areas.

And for the most part the growth of London continued without any kind of planning. The new light industries whose factories could be sited in London because their source of power was not coal but electricity attracted a large population from the distressed areas of the north. The extension of the underground system, the coming of electrification which permitted of more frequent stations because of rapid acceleration, the development of the motor-'bus, and the construction of the arterial roads, all encouraged the further outward sprawl of the metropolis. Between the wars, the built-up area of London doubled, and only in 1935, with the first purchases of land towards the formation of a Green Belt, was any restriction placed on building.

In the centre there were few improvements. No new streets were formed; traffic congestion steadily increased; and many historic buildings, such as the Adelphi, and the aristocratic mansions of Mayfair and St James's, were

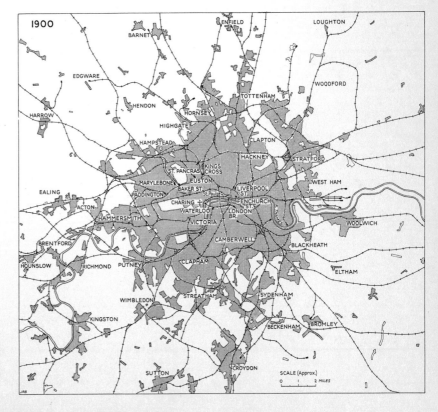

etch map of London at the end of the ctorian age showing the mushroom owth of the suburbs during the nineteenth ntury as a result of fast and cheap mmunications.

demolished to make way for offices, hotels and flats. Flats, first introduced in Victoria Street in the 1850s, now became the accepted mode of dwelling in inner London, and whole streets, Maida Vale and Kensington High Street are instances, were converted into a succession of giant blocks.

Out of the destruction of the Second World War (when much of the City and the East End were razed to the ground) came a determination to build a better London, and comprehensive schemes were prepared for the replanning of the City and the County. These plans, with their recommendations for a series of ring roads (such as had existed in Paris since the nineteenth century), the decentralisation of industry, and the redevelopment of districts that had been crushed into suburbs as living communities, remain the background for present planning, though for various reasons, notably the prohibitive cost of land, they are obviously difficult to implement.

The London County Council embarked on an ambitious programme of housing estates and school building, and began the regeneration of the South Bank. Congestion has been relieved by an extensive reorganisation of the road system (schemes like the Hyde Park Boulevard), and by motorways which reach right into the middle of London, as the arterials of the 1930s did not. Many hundreds of square miles have been added to London's Green Belt, though a high percentage of the population of Greater London now lives beyond it, while over a quarter of a million people have moved out into the New Towns which were created in 1946 to help decentralise the metropolis.

The heart of London has now become to a large extent depopulated; six or seven times more people work in Mayfair and the City than actually live there, and in spite of attempts to decentralise offices, nearly two-thirds of the offices in the whole of Britain remain in central London. Most building in the decade after the war, the period of shortages of materials, was local authority building; most since then has been private development, usually blocks of flats or office buildings. And this has effected a revolution in the appearance of the centre. Before 1956, there were only 16 buildings in London over 150 feet high; now, London is on the way to becoming a skyscraper city.

But mid-twentieth-century London, though in many ways less unified than in any period of its long history, has yet achieved the most unified system of administration it has ever possessed, with the creation in 1963 of the Greater London Council, and the division of powers between it and a smaller number of amalgamated boroughs more clearly defined. Most unified, that is to say, since London ceased, in the later Middle Ages, to be simply the square mile of the City.

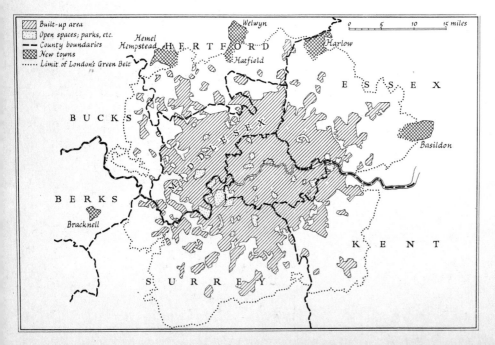

Sketch map of London at the present time, showing the extent of the built-up area beyond the County boundaries.

1 (above)   Much of lowland Britain was covered in thick woodland and marsh in prehistoric times, but the gravel terraces along the Thames, especially on the north bank, provided level, well-drained land where settlement and cultivation were practicable. The streams visible in the distance are the Walbrook and the Fleet.

2 (below)   When London Airport was under construction, archaeological evidence was discovered of an early Iron Age settlement on the site, which contained a large wooden temple and a group of circular huts, surrounded by a stockade.

3 Reconstruction of Roman London before the sack of Boudicca in AD 61. The town had grown up beyond the bridgehead, with a regular system of streets and a number of long straight roads (notably that on the right, which led to Colchester) radiating into the heart of the country. The Fleet river can be seen in the distance.

4 Reconstruction of Roman London in the early second century, showing the development of the port, the size of the forum, the beginnings of settlement across the Walbrook, and the garrison fort recently built at what was later Cripplegate.

5 (above) Reconstruction of Roman London in the third century, showing the defensive walls built at the end of the second century (or perhaps later). The existence of the fort meant that the walls had to follow an irregular course at this point. There is no evidence to suggest that there was ever a wall along the riverfront.

6 (left) Part of the city wall, which was constantly renewed over the centuries. This section rises from the original Kentish ragstone used by the Romans to brick battlements of fifteenth century date. Much of the Roman wall is now buried beneath the 10–12 feet of silt that separates the Roman street level from our own.

7 (right) Reconstruction of Roman Newgate, the main gateway into London on the western side of the city. It is uncertain whether the bastions along the defensive walls, of which one is seen here, were built by the Romans or at a later date, possibly by Alfred in AD 886.

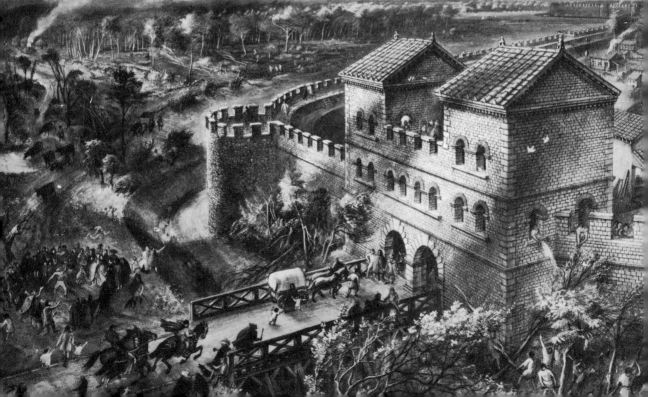

8 (below)   Westminster Abbey, begun by Edward the Confessor in the mid-eleventh century, depicted at the time of his funeral in 1066, before work on the building was quite finished.

9 (bottom)   Westminster Hall, the largest Norman hall in England, remains as a spectacular survival of the palace of the Norman kings, completed by 1099, the 'building beyond compare, with an outwork and bastions' described by Fitz Stephen. The windows and hammer-beam roof are late fourteenth century.

10 The White Tower, the mighty keep built by William the Conqueror on the east of the city to overawe the unruly citizens of London. It was completed by 1100.

¶ Howe Brute buylded London / & called this londe Brytayne / and Scotlonde Albyne / and Walys Camber.

¶ London.

Brute & his men wente forthe and sawe about in dyuers places / where that they myght fynde a good place & couenable / that they myght make a cyte for hym & for his folke. And so at the laste they came by a fayre Ryuer þ is called Tamys / & there Brute began to buylde a fayre Cyte / and lette calle it newe Troy / in mynde & remembraunce of the

11 The earliest printed general view of London, a crude woodcut dating from 1510. Old St Paul's and the Tower are recognisable among the cluster of churches and houses.

12 The Romanesque chancel of St Bartholomew-the-Great, Smithfield, founded in 1123, one of the three great Augustinian priories in London dating from the Norman period.

13 The round nave of the Temple, the church of the Knights Templars, consecrated in 1185. Beyond is the early thirteenth-century chancel.

15 This detail from a famous late fifteenth-century miniature includes the earliest known view of Old London Bridge, which was begun by Peter of Cole-church in 1176 and took about 33 years to complete: notice the superstructure of houses and shops which by this date lined the bridge on both sides, and the flow of water which made it hazardous for small craft to negotiate the arches. The arcaded warehouses of Billingsgate are seen on the right.

16-17 Medieval London had no proper town hall, and civic meetings took place in Aldermanbury (the house of the alderman). With the growing wealth and power of the gilds, the lack of a suitable building was increasingly felt, and Guildhall, with its great hall over 150 feet long, was erected in the early fifteenth century. The hall has now been stripped of its panelling, and is much restored, but one of the lower windows is original. The east part of the crypt beneath has survived intact.

14 (left) The Saxon cathedral of St Paul's was destroyed by fire in 1087, and the opportunity was taken to build its successor on a scale worthy of the rapidly growing importance of London. The great nave, seen here, was built in the twelfth century; the chancel and retrochoir, visible in the distance, were added in the thirteenth century, making the full length of the cathedral almost 600 feet. The spire was nearly 500 feet tall and dominated the city's skyline until its destruction by lightning in 1561.

18 (below) London's wealthiest citizens lived in splendid mansions (known as 'inns' when they were entered through a gatehouse), and Crosby Hall, Bishopsgate, which was built for a rich wool merchant in 1466–75, was reckoned 'verie large and beautifull, and the highest at that time in London'. The house was pulled down at the end of the nineteenth century, but the hall was re-erected in Chelsea.

19 (left) In contrast to such magnificence, most Londoners lived in very cramped surroundings, and these old houses in Cloth Fair, now destroyed, give an accurate impression of the jumbled housing and narrow alleyways characteristic of much of medieval London.

20 (top) Part of the long view of London drawn by Anthony van der Wyngaerde at the end of Henry VIII's reign. The palace of Westminster, with the abbey behind, is seen on the left, and in the centre is the cluster of houses surrounding the court; the pier is a reminder that most traffic was still water-borne. On the right are Charing Cross, the priory of St Mary Rounceval, and St Giles-in-the-Fields.

21 An early view of St James's Palace, built in the 1530s for Henry VIII on the site of a leper hospital in the fields beyond Westminster. The water conduit supplying the palace (which stood nearly on the site of St James's Square) is seen in the centre.

22 By the end of the Tudor period the waterfront between Westminster and the Temple was lined with the mansions of the nobility, each of them with fine gardens running down to the Thames. The first to be built was Somerset House, designed in the Renaissance style in 1547–52 for the Duke of Somerset when he was Lord Protector: this view shows the garden front with the new gallery built in 1661–2. The Dukes of Richmond and Buccleuch were among those who still owned riverside mansions as late as the nineteenth century.

23 Another section of Wyngaerde's long view of London, drawn about 1543–4, showing the Tower and the beginnings of growth outside the walls to the east of the city. The church of St Katharine by the Tower, seen on the right, was demolished when St Katharine's Dock was built in 1825–8.

24 The symbol of London's commercial prosperity and the financial independence of the nation in Elizabethan times was the Royal Exchange, where merchants could meet to transact business in convenient and spacious surroundings. It was built by Sir Thomas Gresham to the designs of a Flemish architect, on a site between Cornhill and Threadneedle Street, in 1566–9.

25 One of the two surviving sections of the earliest map of London known, dating probably from 1558–9. The city ditch is clearly shown, and the name Houndsditch derives (according to Stow) from the dead dogs thrown into it. Ribbon development has begun along Bishopsgate, but to east and west the fields are still the recreational grounds of the citizens: archery can be seen in progress in Finsbury Fields, and on the Spitel (formerly part of the Augustinian priory of St Mary Spital).

Dogge hows.

MOOR FIELD.

Giardin di Piero

MOOR GATE.

All holyes ni the Wall.

The Globe

Beere bay ...

26 (top left) A late nineteenth-century photograph of Staple Inn, Holborn, the most important surviving example of ordinary Elizabethan timber building in London. It shows the overhanging upper storeys, oriel windows and gables characteristic of London houses of the date.

27 (left) A detail from the map illustrated on the preceding page, showing Moorfields. Laundresses are laying out clothes to dry, after washing them in the surrounding streams. The view gives an excellent idea of the pleasant houses and gardens which were characteristic of the outlying parts of London, a contrast to the overcrowding in the centre and in the suburbs.

28 Part of Hollar's famous long view of London, published in 1647, showing the liberties of Southwark. Southwark lay outside the jurisdiction of the City, and was noted for its inns, its bawdy-houses, its prisons, and its theatres (forbidden inside the city). The celebrated Globe Theatre is seen in the distance, and the Bear Garden on the riverfront (Hollar confused the names). In the foreground are the gardens of Winchester House.

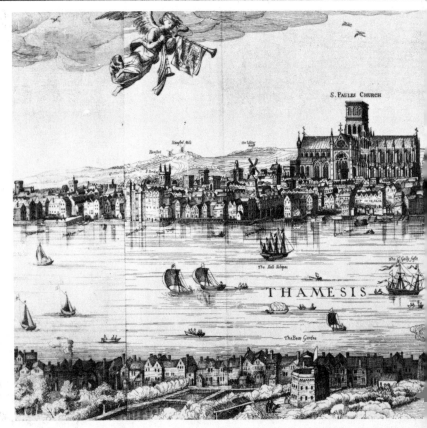

29 London's water supply, hitherto obtained largely from the polluted Thames, was vastly improved in 1613 with the opening of the New River, an artificial waterway over 38 miles long which conducted fresh water from Hertfordshire. The scheme was financed by Sir Hugh Myddelton, and Rosebery Avenue, Islington (close to the site of the original waterhouse at the head of the river, which is seen in this view) is still the headquarters of the Metropolitan Water Board.

30 Visscher's long view of London, published about 1600, though derivative from Norden's view and inexact in many ways, nevertheless gives a vivid impression of the crowded waterfront and of the skyline of spires and steeples; the great spire of Old St Paul's had been destroyed by lightning in 1561, and was never replaced. The Steelyard, until 1598 the enclave of the Hanseatic merchants, can be seen in the centre beneath the church of St Mary-le-Bow.

31-32 (left and below) Details from the earliest painted prospect of London, executed in about 1620–30. The view is taken from above Greenwich, and shows the twin villages of Deptford in the middle distance, with the river winding round towards London. The city was still quite small in actual extent, in spite of its importance and rapidly growing population, and is seen dominated by the massive shapes of Southwark Cathedral and Old St Paul's.

33 (top right) Though Westminster was already overcrowded by the beginning of the seventeenth century, largely with poorer people dependent on employment provided by the court, Tothill Fields remained undeveloped until Cubitt built Belgravia and Pimlico. There were pest-houses in the fields for victims of the plague.

34 (right) London was surrounded by pleasant villages like Hackney or Highgate which were later to be swallowed up in suburban development. Chiswick was a village of mainly Tudor houses, clustered round the church, and this detail from the earliest known view shows Old Corney House, built by the Earl of Bedford, with its delightful garden and Jacobean gazebo overlooking the Thames.

Tootehill fields

St Peter in Westminster · St Paul in London

37 (right) A licence to build 32 houses in the fields behind Lincoln's Inn was granted to a speculator named William Newton in 1638, and two sides of a square were finished by 1641 and occupied by wealthy tenants. The row of houses seen on the right (which Hollar has shown wrongly with plastered façades) was built after the Civil War. Unfortunately only one of the original buildings, Lindsey House, still stands, but the square remains the largest in London.

35 (below) The courtyard of the Earl of Arundel's mansion in the Strand.

Prospect of Linco

36 (left) Covent Garden, the very first square in London, was laid out during the 1630s. There were rows of houses on three sides with arcades beneath (known as the 'piazzas'). This view shows Inigo Jones's church of St Paul's, which stood on the west side. Coaches were now a common sight in the London streets; John Taylor wrote in 1622: 'This is a rattling rowling and rumbling age. The world runs on wheels.'

38 (right) Part of a map of London published in 1658 showing the open space of Lincoln's Inn Fields already surrounded by street development.

...wne, a Troope of Horse & 2 Companies of foote wayted ...garde it & at y.e fall of y.e tope Crosse dromes beat tru- ...ts blew & multitudes ...y.e Ayre. & a greate ...2 of May the Almana: ...the Crosse. & 6 day ...pes burnt, in the pla: ...nginge c.e Bells, & a ...hurt done in all

of Capes warre throwne Shoute of People with ioy, ke fareth, was y.e invention at night was the Leaden :ce where it stood with greate Acclamation & these actions.

39 London was a stronghold of Puritanism during the Civil War. The theatres were closed, sports and games prohibited on Sundays, and symbols of High Church religion defaced: the Cross in Cheapside, one of the 12 Eleanor Crosses erected by Edward I, was destroyed in 1643.

41 (overleaf) The Great Fire of 1666, which raged unchecked for four successive days, and destroyed four-fifths of the city within the walls, was the most tragic event in the whole of London's history. Not only was it a personal disaster for hundreds of thousands of people, but most of London's medieval heritage vanished with the flames. This view shows the scene on the evening of Tuesday, 4 September, when the flames began to engulf Old St Paul's but before its roof collapsed.

40 The overcrowded and insanitary suburbs, which lay outside the jurisdiction of the City, were especially liable to epidemic, and the Great Plague of 1665, in which over 100,000 people died, started in the slums of St Giles-in-the-Fields. Houses marked with a cross (the sign that a victim lay within), the general flight from London, and mass burials, are among the incidents depicted here.

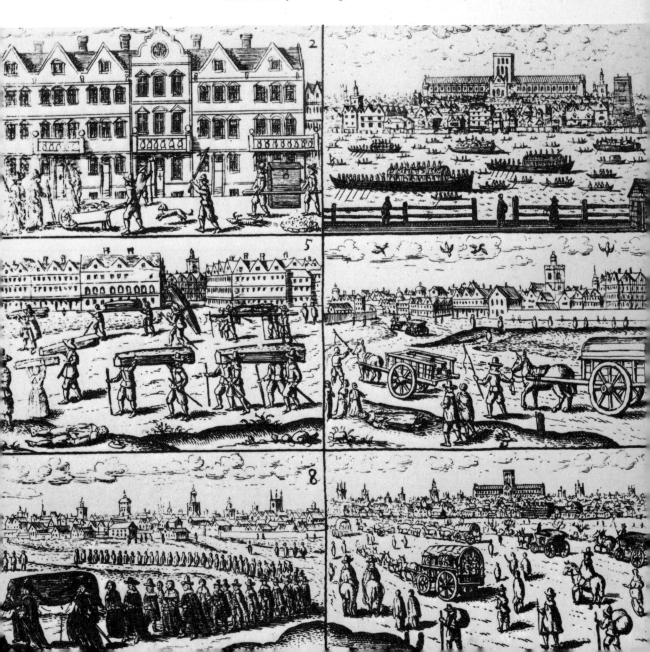

42 The scheme submitted by John Evelyn for reconstructing the city on a more rational street plan. The shaded part (and beyond) denotes the area untouched by the Fire.

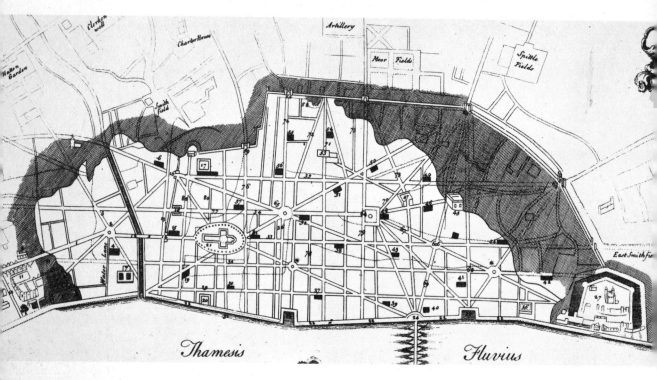

44 St Paul's Cathedral is not only Sir Christopher Wren's masterpiece in architecture, but the greatest building in the classical style in Britain. It was begun in 1675 and finished in 1711. The ground plan is traditional, but Wren's aim was 'to reconcile as near as possible the Gothick to a better Manner of Architecture', and his mighty dome, which dominated London's skyline until comparatively recently, was a worthy rival to St Peter's, Rome.

45 Part of one of the twin towers on the west front of St Paul's, built in 1706–8.

43 (left) A view of Fish Street Hill, showing the regular type of houses, four storeys high in main streets such as this, and built of brick or stone not wood, which were characteristic of the post-Fire City. The Monument, designed by Wren and built in 1671–7, commemorated the place where the Fire broke out.

46 (above)   The interior of St Stephen's, Walbrook, rebuilt by Wren in 1672–7.

47 (top right)   The most splendid of all Wren's steeples, St Mary-le-Bow, completed in 1683.

48 (right)   The Royal Exchange, rebuilt by Edward Jerman, was opened for business in 1671.

49 Coffee-houses, of which there were over 2,000 in London by the end of the seventeenth century, were clubs where people met their friends and business associates and could read the newspapers. Different circles and professions had their favourite rendezvous, and the Stock Exchange, for instance, originated at Jonathan's, a coffee house in 'Change Alley patronised by stockbrokers.

50 The Howland Wet Dock in Limehouse Reach (now the Greenland Dock) was constructed in 1696. The ever increasing trade and traffic of the port was responsible for a rapid growth of population in Stepney and along the riverside eastwards in the later part of the seventeenth century.

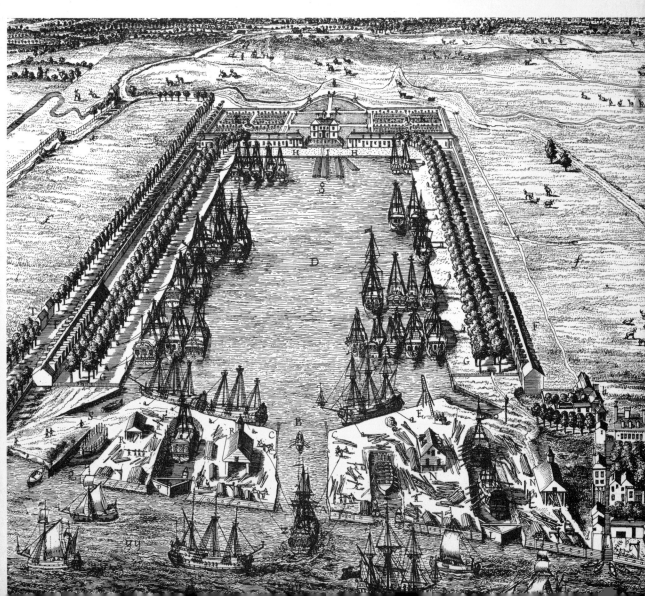

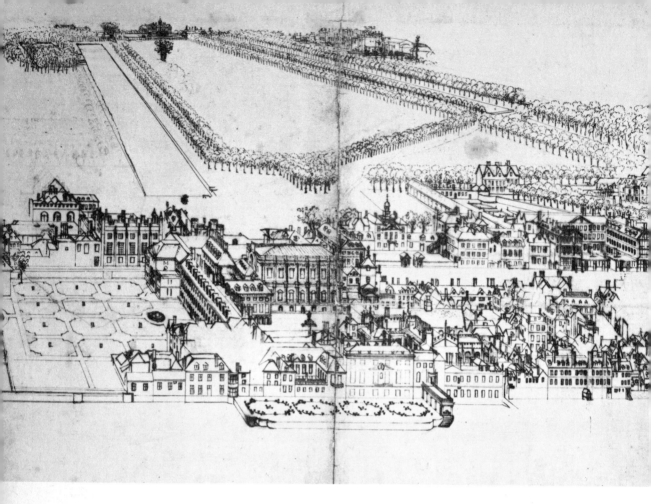

51 (above) A view of Whitehall Palace, the favoured residence of the Tudor and Stuart monarchs, drawn just before its almost total destruction by fire in 1698. The court was then transferred across the Park (laid out in the formal French style for Charles II) to St James's Palace, thus enormously enhancing the social prestige of the newly fashionable quarter of St James's.

52 (below) The scene outside Whitehall Palace on Lord Mayor's Day 1683; the river was still the principal highway of the metropolis.

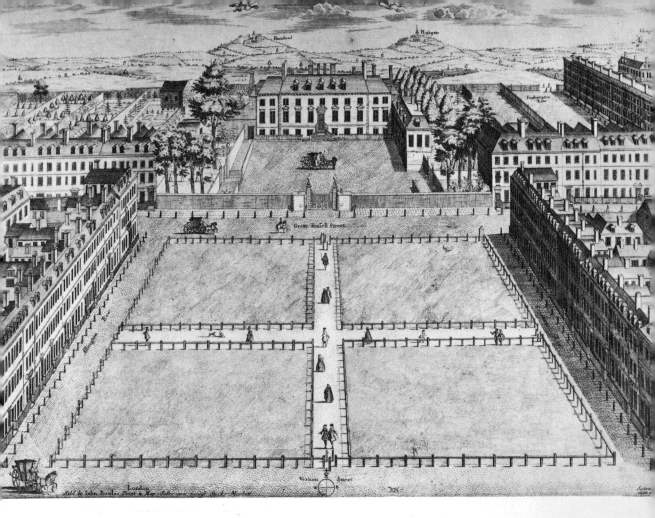

53 (above)   The two most important post-Restoration developments in the West End were in St James's and in Bloomsbury. In 1660 the Earl of Southampton rebuilt his mansion on the outskirts of London, and laid out a fine new square to the south (of which none of the houses now survives). The development was completed by lesser streets surrounding the square and a market, so that Evelyn called it 'a little town'. The hills of Hampstead and Highgate can be seen in the distance.

54 (below)   The mansion built by the Earl of Clarendon on the north side of Piccadilly in 1664–7, which Pepys described as 'the finest pile I ever did see in my life'.

56 In 1725 a newspaper reported that 'there is now building a Square called Grosvenor Square, which for its largeness and beauty will far exceed any yet made in and about London'. In the event it was rather smaller than Lincoln's Inn Fields, but the houses were especially fine, and the architect, Edward Shepherd, even treated a group on the north side to a grand Palladian centrepiece as though they were a single mansion. The square has continued to attract aristocratic residents until the present day.

5 Section of John Rocque's great map of London, published in 1746. An intensive programme of building was carried through on the West End estates in the first half of the eighteenth century, and development stretched as far as Hyde Park on the west and Tiburn Road (Oxford Street) on the north. Cavendish, Hanover, Berkeley and Grosvenor Squares, with their attendant side streets, and in some cases markets and chapels, were all laid out at this time. A brick kiln is marked at the foot of the map.

58 London's shops were reputed to be the finest the world, and for quality, craftsmanship and desi the wares they displayed have probably never be excelled. Assistants were courteous and anxious please, and one foreign visitor wrote that 'the rich merchant never shows ill-humour, even if asked unfold more than a hundred pieces of stuff'. Many the best-known shops were in passages or cou away from the main thoroughfares; Exeter Chan in the Strand, built about 1680, contained 'two wa below stairs, and as many above'.

57 Detail from a view of Holles Street, just off Hanover Square, showing a sedan chair and the fine pavements characteristic of the wealthy residential streets in the West End.

59 Eighteenth-century London was ringed with pleasure gardens of all descriptions. The most celebrated was Vauxhall, opened in 1732, noted for its gay and fashionable décor, its firework displays, and its concerts which were given by the most distinguished singers and instrumentalists of the day. This view shows the supper boxes in part of the grounds.

62 (top right) Crime was rampant, especially in the first half of the eighteenth century; people had to protect themselves and street affrays were a common occurrence. There were also occasional outbreaks of mob violence, notably during the Gordon Riots of 1780.

63 (right) In 1753 Henry Fielding, the novelist, at that time magistrate for Westminster, formed a detachment of thief takers, the celebrated Bow Street runners who were an effective deterrent to crime. Sir John Fielding is seen here presiding over the courtroom at Bow Street.

60 (left) Appalling poverty existed side by side with extreme wealth, and Hogarth's print demonstrated the effects of drinking cheap spirits to which so many of the poor resorted.

61 Government did nothing to improve living conditions, and schools, dispensaries and hospitals were usually started by private philanthropists. The Foundling Hospital, situated (in common with all London hospitals) on what were then the outskirts of the city, was founded in 1739 by Thomas Coram, a retired sea captain.

64 (top left)   One of the problems with which the parish authorities signally failed to deal was the condition of the roads. In the eighteenth century this was remedied by private turnpike trusts, who made a considerable profit from toll charges. This view shows the turnpike and toll-gates at Hyde Park Corner; St George's Hospital is seen on the right.

65 (left)   Smithfield (the smooth field) was already a market, for 'fine horses', in Norman times.

66   It was once a common sight to see cattle being driven through the London streets to Smithfield Market.

67   The New Road (now Marylebone, Euston, Pentonville and City Roads) was begun in 1757. The object was to connect up all the roads converging on London from the north, and to provide a by-pass to the City which could be used by coaches, waggons and drovers going to Smithfield.

69 This print, made at much the same time in 1753, shows the completely rural nature of London's immediate environs. The view is taken from Wandsworth Hill, looking west towards the villages of Putney and Fulham, which were connected by a wooden bridge.

68 This drawing by Canaletto, taken from a little to the north of the New River Head, Islington, shows the extent of London in 1751. The growth of the West End is clearly seen; by contrast, hardly any development has yet begun south of the river.

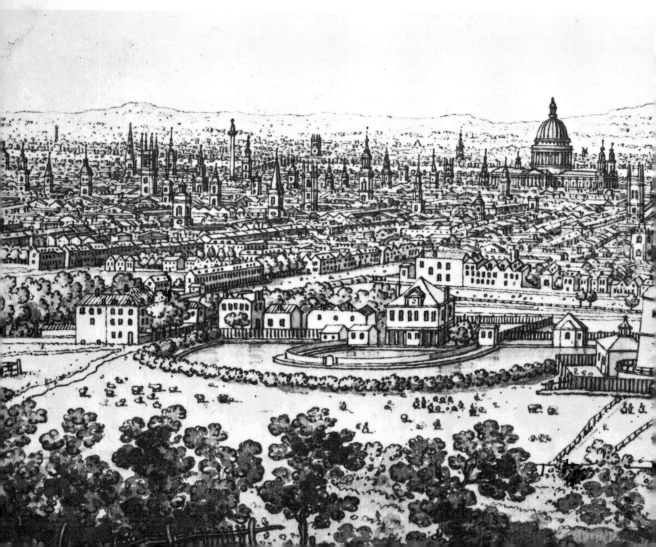

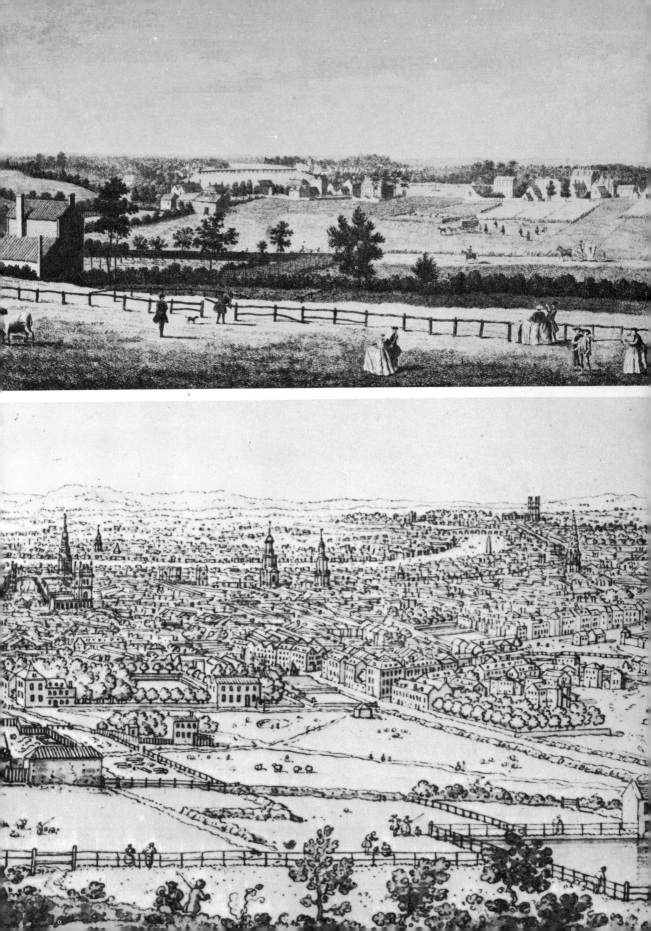

70 Upstream from Putney there was no bridge of any sort until the middle of the eighteenth century. There were innumerable watermen ready to take passengers across in their wherries, but there was only one place to get a coach across, the Horse-ferry from Millbank to Lambeth.

71 Westminster Bridge, designed by a Swiss engineer, Charles Labelye, was opened to traffic in 1750. It was replaced by the present bridge about a century later.

2   Not to be outdone, and anxious to keep traffic flowing into the City, the Corporation planned a new bridge of their own, at Blackfriars, which was designed by Robert Mylne and finished in 1769. This, too, was replaced a century later.

3   The removal of the picturesque but dangerous shop signs, and the substitution of raised pavements for the wooden posts which had formerly divided the footway from the road, were among the many street improvements carried out in the mid-eighteenth century.

74-75 The Stocks Market, a fruit and vegetable market situated where once had been a pair of stocks was closed in 1737, and the Mansion House was built on the site in 1739–53 to provide an official residence for the Lord Mayor. It was ironical that this should have happened at a time when the real power of the City had passed from the gilds and the wards into the hands of the Bank and the new joint-stock companies.

76 (bottom) The city gates (with the exception of Newgate and Temple Bar) were taken down in 1760 to improve the flow of traffic.

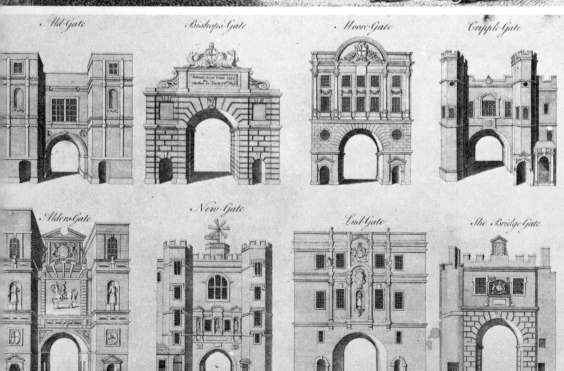

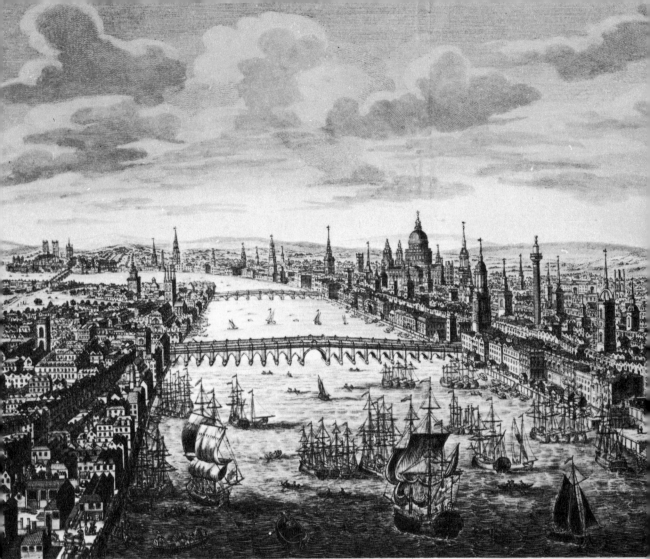

7 The superstructure of medieval houses n London Bridge, which had long been an bstruction to traffic, was removed in 1756; n enlarged central arch was also con-tructed at this time. This view of about 770 shows the two new bridges, with Westminster Bridge Road little more than country track winding across St George's Fields.

8 Part of a map of 1784 showing the oads which were built across the marshes rom the new bridges, converging at St George's Circus. South London was at last pen to development. The horseferry can e seen in the corner of the map.

79 The Adelphi was one of the most spectacular of eighteenth-century developments. Planned by the Brothers Adam, its principal feature was the beautiful Royal Terrace overlooking the river, which was horribly altered in 1872 and finally, in 1937, demolished completely.

80 (top) The villages round London were now attracting more residents and terraces of houses began to stretch out into what was formerly farmland. This view shows the terraces built in the 1770s on the Canonbury House estate, well beyond the New Road.

81 Eighteenth-century London was ringed with the kilns and works and yards attendant on the building industry. Timber yards stretched the length of the south bank. This watercolour shows tile kilns in Bagnigge Wells Road, in the neighbourhood of King's Cross. The stream is part of the Fleet Ditch.

82 Masquerades were held frequently both at Ranelagh and at Vauxhall Gardens, and a young lady dressed as a shepherdess is shown returning in a sedan chair exhausted from the night's revels.

83 Bagnigge Wells was better known for its much frequented tea garden which had a bowling green and skittle alley.

84 In the second half of the eighteenth century, many of the more popular coffee houses were turned into subscription clubs. This view of St James's Street shows Boodle's Club, built in 1765 (on the left), and Brooks's, which dates from 1788 (on the right).

86 The East India Company, which was the richest of all the great joint-stock enterprises, built a fine new headquarters for itself in Leadenhall Street in 1797–1800.

85 (left) The Bank of England, founded in 1694, was rebuilt by
Sir John Soane at the end of the eighteenth century. By this date
there were over 60 banking firms in London, most of them started by
wealthy goldsmiths.

87 In this picture of one of the so-called 'legal quays', possibly
Bear Quay, a customs officer is questioning a ship's captain about
the contents of his cargo.

88 Every ship's cargo entering or leaving the Port of London had to be handled at one of the 'legal quays', between the Tower and London Bridge. This caused so much congestion in the Pool, and dislocation at the quayside, in the last decade of the eighteenth century when the volume of trade doubled, that an alternative system became an imperative need.

89 In 1799 Parliament approved the construction of a great new complex of docks, and the West India Dock, on the Isle of Dogs, was the first to be completed. The London Dock, seen here, which was built in Wapping at a cost of two million pounds, was opened to shipping in 1805.

90-91 (above) Regent's Canal was constructed in 1812-20 continue the Grand Union Canal as far as the Thames at Limehous The junction of the two canals was made in Paddington, at what w then the very edge of London's built-up area (this is now the distri called 'Little Venice').

92 (top right) Several arterial roads by-passing Islington and t northern heights were constructed under turnpike schemes at t period. The Archway Road, which was one of the earliest, dati from 1812, by-passed Highgate on the east side and provided easier gradient for traffic; the Archway itself was built over t road in 1813.

93 A view of Ludgate Hill showing a stage coach leaving the Be Sauvage inn for Cambridge.

95 The old Elephant and Castle inn was pulled down in 1818, and replaced by a fine new coaching inn which soon became the most popular stage for travellers passing through south London on their way to and from Brighton.

94 The Elephant and Castle first became an important junction when London Road was built southwards from St George's Circus and this was joined by the New Kent Road. The inn was originally a smithy, and only converted into a hostelry at this date.

96 The most distinguished street improvement ever carried out in London was Nash's 'royal mile' from the Prince Regent's palace of Carlton House to the Regent's Park. It was built in 1812–28 on slum property bordering on Mayfair. This view shows the magnificent sweep of the Quadrant.

97 (bottom) A view higher up Regent Street showing the elegance and variety of its original architecture.

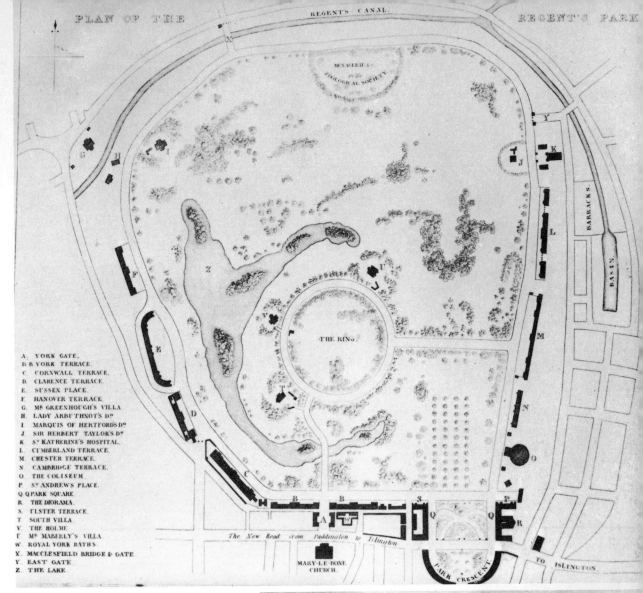

MENAGERIE of the ZOOLOGICAL SOCIETY

THE RING.

BARRACKS

BASIN

A. YORK GATE.
B B. YORK TERRACE.
C. CORNWALL TERRACE.
D. CLARENCE TERRACE.
E. SUSSEX PLACE.
F. HANOVER TERRACE.
G. Mr GREENHOUGH'S VILLA
H. LADY ARBUTHNOT'S Do
I. MARQUIS OF HERTFORD'S Do
J. SIR HERBERT TAYLOR'S Do
K. St KATHERINE'S HOSPITAL.
L. CUMBERLAND TERRACE.
M. CHESTER TERRACE.
N. CAMBRIDGE TERRACE.
O. THE COLISEUM
P. St ANDREWS PLACE.
Q Q PARK SQUARE.
R. THE DIORAMA.
S. ULSTER TERRACE.
T. SOUTH VILLA.
V. THE HOLME.
U. Mr MABERLY'S VILLA
W. ROYAL YORK BATHS.
X. MACCLESFIELD BRIDGE & GATE.
Y. EAST GATE.
Z. THE LAKE.

The New Road from Paddington to Islington

MARY-LE-BONE CHURCH.

PARK CRESCENT

TO ISLINGTON

98 Plan of Regent's Park, showing the picturesque layout of the lake and trees, the scattered villas, and the imposing terraces surrounding. Park Crescent was the termination of Regent Street.

99 Park Village East, begun in 1824, one of the two groups of more modest villas which Nash planned to the east of Regent's Park. This type of development profoundly influenced the planning of the Victorian suburbs.

100 (top) Communications south of the river were further improved at this period by three new bridges, Vauxhall, Waterloo and Southwark. Waterloo Bridge, seen here, was built by Sir John Rennie, and finished in 1817. It was replaced by the present structure in 1945.

101 These villas on Herne Hill are a pleasant example of the wealthier houses which now began to rise in suburbs like Clapham and Camberwell, in addition to the familiar terrace development.

102 Regency London was noted for the elegance of its fashions, and the Burlington Arcade, built in 1815–9, was occupied (then as now) by hosiers, glovers, hatters and similar shops.

103 The Hyde Park Corner Screen, built by Decimus Burton in 1825, one of the most striking surviving monuments to Regency London, was originally planned in conjunction with the Constitution Arch as a grand entrance to Nash's new Buckingham Palace.

105 A general view of the City in 1840, showing its appearance at the beginning of the Victorian age. Farringdon and New Bridge Streets stretch across the foreground, with Ludgate Hill leading to St Paul's. The Fleet and Newgate prisons are prominent on the left, while New London and Southwark Bridges can be seen on the right.

4 George Shillibeer's omnibus, which was introduced in 1829 d plied from Paddington to the Bank via the Angel, was not quite revolutionary a vehicle as is usually maintained, since in type it s only a development of the long stagecoach that had been on the eets for about 30 years. What was really new about the omnibus s that it catered specifically for passengers making short journeys.

106 Millbank remained a pleasant riverside walk from Westminster to Chelsea until the beginning of Queen Victoria's reign.

107 The turnpike at Croydon, which remained a country village until the 1840s, and was only absorbed in the built-up area of the metropolis at the beginning of the present century.

108 In 1740 a guide to London had described the Thames-side villages as 'full of beautiful buildings, being country houses of noblemen, gentlemen, and indeed tradesmen of the City of London'. The riverside (especially near Twickenham and Richmond) was still lined with wealthy retreats in the early nineteenth century. This villa was the seat of the Earl of Cassillis.

109 Brentford, on the main road to the west, was a quiet early Georgian village with a pretty market square.

111 The earliest main-line railway was the London and Birmingham, opened in 1837. This view shows the terminus at Euston, the first of London's great stations to be built (London Bridge was its only predecessor).

0 (left) The London and Greenwich was the first of London's
railways, the line being opened from Deptford to Bermondsey (and
later London Bridge) in 1836. The railway was raised above the
adjacent property (chiefly market gardens) on a long viaduct, part
of which is seen here.

2 In spite of initial opposition from the City, the London and
Blackwall Railway was allowed to take its line inside the boundaries
as far as Fenchurch Street. The City subsequently decided not to
allow other railways north of the river a similar privilege, and the
new Fenchurch Street terminus, built in 1853, was designed to
accommodate the lines which other companies operating to the
north and east of London wanted to bring into the heart of the City.

113 This placid view of Wandsworth, drawn from Putney Bridge in 1837, shows how the rural nature of the Thames-side close to London persisted well into the nineteenth century: most of this area was still devoted to market gardening.

114 During the Victorian period, London's water-front became increasingly industrialised. This view, taken about 1845–50, shows part of Cubitt's works in the immediate foreground, with distilleries and waterworks behind; on the Battersea shore is the engine house of the Southwark and Vauxhall Water-works, with Battersea Fields beyond. Battersea Bridge can be seen in the distance.

115 Belgrave Square, laid out after 1825 as part of Cubitt's large-scale development in this area, extends over ten acres and was the most impressive rival to Nash's terraces round Regent Park.

116 (bottom) The development of Paddington and Bayswater began in 1827, and by mid-century most of this area had been built up with stuccoed terraces, squares and crescents. In 1831 the population was only 6,500, but by 1851, when Paddington Station was building, it had risen to 46,000. Westbourne Terrace, seen here, one of the grandest of the new streets, was laid out in 1847–52.

117 Buckingham Street, off the Strand, typical of many of the side
streets of mid-Victorian London. In the distance can be seen the
York Water Gate and one of the towers of Brunel's elegant Hungerford Suspension Bridge (destroyed in 1859–60 to make way for the
Charing Cross railway bridge). Two of Nicholas Barbon's original
late seventeenth-century houses still survive.

118 (left) The Great Exhibition of the Works of Industry of all Nations was opened in the specially built 'Crystal Palace' in Hyde Park on 1 May 1851. In the six months before November, when it was closed, over six million people visited the exhibition.

119 (bottom left) A view of the Bank intersection showing the increasing congestion of the City streets in the early Victorian period. A hansom cab is seen in the centre, and the new type of omnibus, which had a longitudinal seat (known as a 'knifeboard') installed on top, is much in evidence. London's bus services expanded enormously as a result of the great influx of visitors to the Great Exhibition, and the London General Omnibus Company was formed in 1855.

120 This print gives some idea of the crowds which daily surged over New London Bridge in Victorian times. The traffic was often so dense that omnibuses could be held up for 20 minutes.

121   Crowds at Paddington Station in 1862.

122 Penge is an example of one of the outer suburbs, with imposing villas for the wealthy and streets of terrace or semi-detached houses, that grew up round the newly built railway stations.

123 These streets of terrace houses in Penge, with their debased Gothic or classical detail, are typical of much suburban development in the later Victorian period.

124 Wealthier people lived in villas set in their own grounds. The red brick and medieval tower of this house in Melbury Road, Kensington, built in the 1870s for his own occupation by the architect William Burges, are characteristic of the late nineteenth-century reaction against stuccoed symmetry and formalism.

125 The Metropolitan Railway, the first underground railway in the world, was designed to ease the traffic congestion in the streets above. Opened in 1863, it ran from Paddington to Farringdon Street, and connected three of London's main-line termini.

126   The railways, which proliferated in south London and began to thrust over the river in the 1860s to termini on the north bank, caused large areas in the suburbs of Bermondsey, Southwark and Lambeth to degenerate into slums.

127 Sir Joseph Bazalgette, Engineer to the Metropolitan Board of Works, planned and constructed in 1859–66 an entirely new system of main drainage for London, with outfalls well below the city so that sewage was no longer deposited into the Thames at London. This view shows the construction of the Abbey Mills pumping station at West Ham.

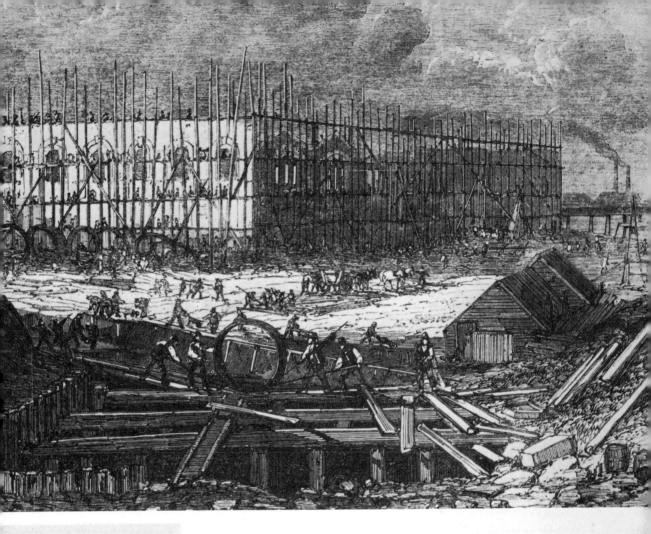

128 The Victoria Embankment, which stretches from Westminster to Blackfriars, was also constructed by Bazalgette in 1864–70. This wide new thoroughfare considerably improved the flow of traffic.

131 (top right) A frighteningly high p
portion of London's population contin
to live in conditions of dire poverty, o
partially relieved by private philanthro
The Salvation Army was founded in
same decade as this picture was paint
the 1870s.

132 (bottom right) An example of me
early nineteenth-century terrace housing
Southwark which had become a compl
slum by the end of the century. The sa
process of degeneration is continuing tod
in districts such as Kilburn.

129 The first serious attempt to provide
better homes for the poorer classes dates
from the 1860s. A sum of half a million
pounds donated to the City of London by
George Peabody, an American banker, was
devoted to building blocks of working-class
flats; Peabody Square in Blackfriars Road,
seen here, was the first to be planned, in
1862. The institutional character of these
flats betrays the Victorian attitude towards
the less fortunate.

130 Victoria Park, which is partly in
Hackney and partly in Bethnal Green, was
planned as a large open space for the
recreation of poorer people in the East End.
It was opened in 1845. Among the many
facilities subsequently provided were swim-
ming pools, gymnasia and cricket pitches.

133 (left) Another innovation in Victori[an]
transport was the tram, first introduced [in]
London by an American entrepreneur [in]
1861. Parliament prohibited tramways [in]
the centre of the city (their rails w[ere]
regarded as an obstruction to traffic) a[nd]
the tram companies operated chiefly [in]
north London. This picture shows a tr[am]
on Pentonville Hill, which was so steep th[at]
three horses had to be employed.

134 The crowded Strand at the end of [the]
Victorian era.

135 Picturesque but often unsavoury courts and passages in which it was easy for the uninitiated to lose their way were still characteristic of London's haphazard topography. This etching shows the entrance to Clare Market, between Lincoln's Inn and the Strand, an area of mean streets, with a somewhat sinister reputation, which was later cleared for the construction of Kingsway.

136 The broad tree-lined avenues of Aldwych and Kingsway, laid out in the Edwardian period, were the last significant street improvements carried out in central London until recent years.

137 Albert Hall Mansions, designed by Norman Shaw in 1879, was the first block of flats to be built in London, and marks the beginnings of a radical change in the way of living of the wealthier classes.

138 Hampstead Garden Suburb was begun in 1907. This aerial view shows the central square, which was planned as a social centre, the deliberately irregular street pattern, and the woods and trees that were retained in the layout.

139 In this view of London taken from Parliament Hill Fields in
the 1920s, St Paul's still dominates the skyline much as it had done
in Canaletto's time. But the indications of grime and soot provided
by the smoking chimneys are in contrast with the cleaner air
characteristic of most of eighteenth-century London.

140 Another view of the same date showing crowds walking
work across Blackfriars Bridge, and the electric trams that then ra
along the Embankment. Prominent along the riverside skyline a
the towers of the Houses of Parliament, the shot tower that stood c
the south bank until 1962, and the pinnacles of Whitehall Court,
late Victorian block of flats.

144 (above) St Paul's enveloped by smoke during the air raid of 29 December 1940. Though a large part of the City was devastated by bombs, the Cathedral remained miraculously unharmed.

141 (top left) The development of light industry and long rows of mock-Tudor semi-detached houses along the Great West Road in the 1920s.

142 The rapid growth of housing estates in Edgware in the late 1920s was due entirely to the extension of the Northern Line. Edgware tube station, built in 1925, can be seen in the right foreground.

143 London County Council flats built at the White City in the later 1930s. Wealthy blocks of pre-war flats, such as Dolphin Square, were similarly uninspired in layout.

147 (right) Among the most importa[nt] improvements in communications in t[he] 1960s were the motorways which we[re] gradually extended into the centre [of] London. This is part of the West Cr[oss] Route, looking southwards from Ear[l's] Court.

148 (bottom right) Housing developme[nt] at Croxley Green in Hertfordshire, showi[ng] the limits of the built-up area of Grea[ter] London and part of the statutory Gre[en] Belt intended to prevent further outwa[rd] sprawl. The West Hertfordshire golf cour[se] is seen in the distance, and Whippend[ell] Wood lies a little to the north.

145   The paramount need in the post-war years was for new houses and new schools. A high standard of architecture was set by the London County Council, and among its best and most varied housing estates were those in the Putney-Roehampton area, where the slopes and numerous trees provided natural picturesque advantages. The Alton West estate, seen here, was built at the end of the 1950s.

146   In the ten years following the war the streets of central London became increasingly congested, and this cartoon by Fougasse suggests something of the general despair that any permanent solution could ever be found.

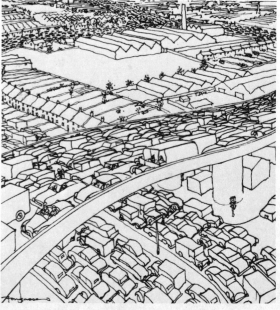

152 (right) Perhaps the most revolutionary change of all in post-war London has been the coming of the skyscraper, which has totally altered the historic skyline. One of the most distinguished architecturally is the Vickers Building on Millbank.

149 The south bank between Waterloo Bridge and the County Hall, which had become increasingly depressed in the nineteenth century, was replanned after the war as a cultural centre. The first building to rise was the Royal Festival Hall, opened in 1951; this view shows the Queen Elizabeth Hall and Purcell Room, opened in 1967, with Big Ben and Adelphi House in the distance.

150-151 (below) The Elephant and Castle is one of the many important road junctions in central London and the inner suburbs to be completely redesigned. Pedestrian subways are an integral part of their planning.

153   A view of the City in 1967 showing a multi-storey car park in the foreground, and the mushroom growth of high office blocks, almost dwarfing the spires and steeples of Wren's churches. St Mary-le-Bow, seen upper left, is still prominent, though hemmed in.

Index

Numerals in italics refer to the figure-numbers of the illustrations